Understanding Unreasonable Force

The use of Force with Children & Young People

"It is difficult to get a man to understand something when his salary depends on him not understanding it."

Mark Dawes

&

Deborah Jones

The Derwent Press
Derbyshire, England
www.derwentpress.com

UNDERSTANDING UNREASONABLE FORCE
by
Mark Dawes and Deborah Jones

ISBN 10:   1-84667-030-6
ISBN 13:   978-1-84667-030-5

Book design by:
Pam Marin-Kingsley, www.far-angel.com

Published in 2008
by
The Derwent Press
Derbyshire, England
www.derwentpress.com

Dedication

To Ashley South (17th October 1976 – 8th September 2000): A young man committed to helping children and who was an inspiration to many others, both young and old. 'There is no Justice higher than the Truth.'

This book has to also be primarily dedicated to Deborah and Alan Jones, whose knowledge, tenacity, patience and unselfish support over the years have led to the publishing of this book. Without Deborah and Alan's input, our professional expertise in this area would never have evolved to the degree that it is at now.

It is also dedicated to every child in our society who has the right to live their lives free from unnecessary harm, pain and the unnecessary needless risk of death from the use of physical force imposed upon them by the very institutions mandated to care for them that they may find themselves in.

This book is also dedicated to the many hard-working staff who themselves dedicate their lives to the welfare of the children in their care, whose work and commitment generally goes unrecognised and unrewarded. They provide a valuable and vitally important service and who too should be expected to provide that service free from the risk of harm and death.

We would also like to dedicate this book to those who have trained with us over the years. Your input and feedback on our courses has enabled us to reflect on what we do and how we do it. Without this valuable feedback, we would not have been able to move forward in the right direction. You make us better than we know we can be.

It is finally dedicated to you, the reader, who by deciding to pick up this book has taken a decisive step forward in wanting to improve your judgement, knowledge and skill.

Contents

Preface

The use of force with children and young people is an emotive subject. It is a subject fraught with controversy and at times, built on myth and misinterpretation. This in itself gives rise to the paradox that exists in our schools, care homes and secure establishments, where the very systems and policies put in place to protect children by well-meaning adults can sometimes expose children to even greater risk.

It's fair to say that children and young people are among some of the most vulnerable groups in our society, highlighted and illustrated by the past enquiries that uncovered large scale abuse of children in residential care. However, within this vulnerable sector are also some of the most violent children, and this is something we also need to consider when tasking staff with their control and safety, particularly when determining any use of physical force policy for either the protection of children or the staff employed to look after them.

For example, many staff in some agencies believe that they are not allowed to use physical force to prevent a child who may be about to abscond from doing so as they believe that this is in some way 'against the law', yet the very same agency will contact the police who will, if necessary, use lawful force to bring the child back to the place he or she has absconded from.

Many agencies only use systems of restraint based solely on the use of non-restrictive or non-pain compliance techniques, commonly known as 'non-harmful methods of control', because they have been led to believe that any technique that causes discomfort or pain is 'against the law'.

School staff now have lawful authority to stop and search pupils for knives and other weapons, remove the weapons, and, if necessary—use physical force to do so. Remember Philip Lawrence who was stabbed to death outside the gates of his school in December 1995 when he went to the aid of a pupil who was being attacked by a gang? Remember Stephen Lawrence, the young teenager stabbed to death and Damilola Taylor, who was left to die in a stair well.

Ask the police to deal with a knife incident and you will get either an armed response unit, officers armed with tazers, or as a minimal response, a support unit equipped with body armour, batons, CS-spray, handcuffs and shields. So why is it perceived that it is apparently 'against the law' for some staff to use force, or more restrictive techniques, when it is lawful for other members of the public (for example, a member of the public who is a constable) to do so?

These questions give rise to the paradox that exists in our society today, where the very systems and policies put in place to protect children by well-meaning adults could actually be placing the child, other children, and indeed the staff member, at an increased risk of harm.

In this book we will delve into the 'taboo' that is the intentional use of pain when attempting to restrain a child/young person and we will then place an argument at your feet—that in certain circumstances the use of pain is not only acceptable but also, in some circumstances, absolutely necessary if we are to act in the best interests of the child and others, including the staff employed to care for them.

This book also provides some analysis of how these issues may be addressed in policy and practice. It aims, therefore, to dispel myths and misunderstandings that exist by looking squarely at the facts, so that you will be better informed and more competent in carrying out your professional duties, and be better placed to achieve the ultimate aim, the protection of children and young people in our care. This book will also explore how the use of physical restraint should be planned and considered by responsible managers and appointed agents of the Government.

In essence, this book aims to highlight some of the key issues in relation to physical interventions with children and young people as well as providing a resource and reference point for practitioners.

However, even today, in the minds of many professionals, such as child protection social workers, there is no such thing as the reasonable use of force. Force per se is always considered unreasonable, hence the title of the book—Understanding Unreasonable Force.

Chapter 1
The Risks

Part 1: The Risk Posed to Children & Young People

During the 1990's there was a considerable increase in concern about the abuse of children in residential care, with ten public enquiries between 1990 and 1996 that exposed the large-scale physical, emotional and sexual abuse of many of the most vulnerable children in our care system.

With regards to physical abuse, there was specific concern about children receiving severe injuries whilst being inappropriately restrained. At Ayclife, for example (a secure Children's Unit in County Durham), where staff had been trained in control and restraint techniques by prison service trainers, it was alleged that several children had suffered broken bones whilst being physically restrained. A subsequent inquiry however, by the Social Services Inspectorate in 1993, revealed that a number of these injuries had been sustained prior to the training being introduced and established no links between the two. Nonetheless, the potential for abuse of such techniques was evident, and sadly one does not have to look far to find appalling instances of abuse of vulnerable people.

In 1991 the PINDOWN report was also published. The Pindown regime, used in Staffordshire children's homes, was a crude method of controlling children with behavioural problems. It was fundamentally a form of solitary confinement based on sensory deprivation. The youngest child subjected to this regime was said to have been 9 years old. At its longest, the technique was used for up to 84 consecutive days, which the inquiry found it to be extremely abusive.

The Department of Health responded by commissioning the Utting Report (1991), which concluded that the implementation of the Children Act 1989 was enough to prevent the likes of "Pindown" happening again.

The Utting Report in 1997 also considered children spending long periods in hospitals and boarding schools. It stressed that measures were to be put in place to ensure greater safety for children, e.g. improved vetting of staff and whistle-blowing procedures. The Utting Report highlighted how alarmingly easy it was for the care and control of vulnerable or difficult children to slip over into abuse, with harsh regimes and over-punitive methods being exploited by those intent on abuse. Research by Berridge and Broudie indicated that staff concern about how to control children's behaviour in residential care is "undoubtedly a major pre-occupation" for those employed on the units (Berridge and Broudie, 1998).

This was followed by the Lost in Care report from the Waterhouse tribunal, the largest child abuse inquiry ever set up in the UK, which heard evidence from hundreds of victims, highlighting abuse in children's homes in North Wales.

Following on from these enquiries, Government departments have issued extensive guidance and regulations aimed at clarifying the situation regarding physical interventions with children and young people. Frequently, however, it has created rather than dispelled confusion in this area, much of the confusion arising from the focus of advice being on what staff could not do, as opposed to what they could, providing little assistance for staff in terms of dealing with more extreme challenging behaviour.

However, in spite of the laws, guidance, and regulations, children are still being injured and killed as the recent high profile case of the death of 15 year-old Gareth Myatt clearly illustrated.

For another child, Adam Rickwood, the youngest child ever to die in penal custody in the UK, it was his refusal to go to his room that led to a restraint which resulted in him taking his own life.

Adam was found hanging in his room in Hassockfield Secure Training Centre at around midnight on 9th August 2004. In the hours preceding his death, he was subjected to restraint by four male officers. During the restraint, it was recorded that a *"nose distraction"* technique, described as a *"karate-like chop"* to his nose, had been used on him. This was said to have caused Adam to have a nose-bleed for an hour. There was no suggestion that any of the criteria set out in the Secure Training Centre Rules had been met that could have justified Adam's restraint. After his death a "statement" was found in his room in which he described in his own words what had happened to him:

"My [Adam Rickwood's] *Statement* [to the authorities]

On the 8th August at approx 6.50pm, I was sat at the table on the wing 2 Bravo. And my friend was messing about, so he was put in his cell for 30 minutes (time out). When my friend was in his cell he asked me to go over to his door. When I went over he slid a piece of paper under the door and asked me to give it to a female member of staff.

When I gave the paper to her she told me to get in my room. I asked why and she said 'Just go in' then at that point I refused because there were no explicit reason for this. Then she called for first response (assistance from other staff). When the other staff came they all jumped on me and started to put my arms up my back and hitting me in the nose. I then tried to bite one of the staff because they were really hurting my nose. My nose started bleeding and swelled up and it didn't stop bleeding for about one hour and afterwards it was really sore. When I calmed down I asked them why they hit me in the nose and jumped on me. They said it was because I wouldn't go in my room so I said what gives them the right to hit a 14 year-old child in the nose and they said it was restraint."

In 2003, the year before Adam Rickwood died, staff at Hassockfield, which holds 40 children, had used restraint 972 times![1] That equates to 24.3 restraints per child per year or 81 restraints a month! Between November 2005 and October 2006 restraint was used 3036 times in Secure Training Centres that hold a total of 240 children[2].

Today in our modern so called 'civilised' society, children who are likely to be restrained are still as vulnerable as they were when the public enquiries first uncovered the large-scale abuse of children in residential care, and the specific concerns about children receiving severe injuries whilst being inappropriately restrained are still as valid today as they were all those years ago. Yet history still seems to repeat itself.

As a result, the physical restraint of children and young people continues to be a sensitive and emotive issue.

For those required to carry out restraint, there is often confusion about when it is appropriate and how it should be done. Concern about possible consequences, such as injury to the child.

---

1 INQUEST briefing on the restraint of children and SI 2007 No 1709 regarding changes to the Secure Training Centre Rules

2 Lords written answers nos. HL560-563 12 December 2006.

For those staff commissioned to "buy in" training, the past history of abuse, the wide and diverse range of statute and common law expected to be complied with and the lack of specific regulation and limited empirical research with regard to the use of physical force, all add up to make this a daunting task.

Physical restraint should always be a last resort and not a primary source of intervention. In much of the literature concerning care and control of children and young people, emphasis is quite rightly placed upon avoiding the need for physical intervention and looking at alternatives such as the imposition of sanctions, boundary setting, teaching consequences and positive re-enforcement, and conflict management. It follows therefore that physical skills training should not be taught in isolation, but as part of a larger programme that provides staff with other skills.

If a competent risk assessment identifies that physical restraint training is necessary, then staff must also develop a clear understanding of the legal context in which physical interventions may be used, as it is not the technique alone which renders restraint reasonable or otherwise, but the circumstances in which it is applied. For example, without lawful excuse, firm grips on the arms of a child which restrict their movement may be unreasonable, e.g. if applied simply because they would not comply with a particular staff instruction. However, a high degree of force may well be reasonable and necessary in some situations, e.g. where there is a risk of serious imminent danger.

As a result of historical abuse and the numerous enquiries into the same, all legislation rightly promotes the principle that in all our interactions relating to children and young people the child's welfare must be at the forefront of our thinking. However, in considering this legislative principle, we also need to acknowledge that amongst some of the most vulnerable and damaged children and young people in our society, there are also

17

some of the most potentially dangerous. Therefore, consideration of any physical intervention in potentially volatile situations requires an understanding of the risks involved to all concerned. It also requires a competent understanding and practical knowledge of how to apply physical intervention in such a way as to reduce or minimise such risks in line with current legislation.

It is fair to point out at this stage that many Departmental Regulations, Codes of Practice and indeed, even Acts of Parliament, would seem to contradict one another, so a broad and deep grasp has to be sought of a wide range of legislation, as well as the hierarchy of what overrides what—a daunting task!

However, if staff are not taught physical skills within a competent legal framework and without an understanding of the risks involved, they are likely to lack confidence in using the techniques they have been taught, be fearful of the consequences and, as a result, restraint may not occur on occasions when it should and may also occur on occasions when it should not.

Part 2: The Risk Posed by Children & Young People

So far we have considered children and young people in terms of their vulnerability, but there is another important consideration that should not be overlooked, which is the risk children and young people pose to those expected to care for them.

Recent Home Office published figures in December 2005 showed that a quarter of all people arrested in England and Wales were juveniles. This equated to an increase of 10 per cent in 2 years. Of these juveniles arrested, 23 per cent were for violent offences and 70 per cent were re-convicted within 2 years. What was also alarming was that arrests of young women soared by 80 per cent in 5 years.

In 1999 The British Crime Survey reported that about a sixth (16 per cent) of physical assaults at work involved offenders under the age of 16, and that most of the incidents involving young people were against teachers and other education and welfare workers.

Furthermore, the Health and Safety Executive recently reported that violent assaults on teachers have risen by a third despite attempts to clamp down on poor behaviour. The HSE reported that twice as many teachers suffered such severe injuries that they needed to be resuscitated or kept in hospital. This resulted in an increase from 205 in 2003 to 272 in 2004 in the number of teachers in England who had to take at least three days off work because of attacks at school. The findings also showed that the number of teachers with major injuries, including amputations, fractures and dislocated joints, doubled from 27 to 55. The HSE's figures mostly represent injuries to teachers and classroom assistants but include attacks on a handful of other school staff such as school secretaries and caretakers. However, secondary teachers were the most likely to be attacked, followed by secondary teaching assistants, primary assistants and then primary teachers.

In addition to the HSE's own figures, recent cases that have been reported in the press also highlight the growing risk to teachers, and the following are some of the most recent.

"A teacher from Staffordshire who suffered such a serious back injury in the assault at a secure unit that she could not work again has been awarded £402,000 from the Criminal Injuries Compensation Authority is thought to be the biggest in the union's history[3].

---

3 As reported by the BBC on 7th September 2007

Another teacher, a member of the NASUWT, received £165,000 from Leeds City Council after being injured repeatedly while trying to break up fights at a rough city school. She said she felt she had to intervene in a fight in which a group of white boys trapped one Pakistani 13 year-old and started punching him in the face. While asking to remain anonymous, she told the TES (the Times Educational Supplement): "It's hard when you've had the confidence knocked out of you mentally and physically."

In another case a teacher won £330,000 after quitting her job at a Birmingham special school after being threatened by a thug. The massive sum handed to Anna Mongey in an out-of-court settlement is believed to be the largest paid by the authority to an employee in recent years. She sued the council after the intruder, understood to have been freed a short time earlier from a jail sentence, confronted her at Lindsworth Special School in Monyhull Hall Road, Kings Norton. Ms Mongey ordered him out of her class but he threatened to return for her. She was not hurt but never returned to her job and launched legal action believed to relate to risk assessment procedures. The National Union of Teachers today hailed the settlement and called on heads to protect their staff."

[4]*"A teacher attacked by a dangerous pupil won £190,000 high court damages yesterday in what lawyers said was the first reported case in which a local authority was held liable for failing to protect a teacher. Judith Waugh, head of the lower school at John F Kennedy special school in Stratford, east London, had received glowing assessments*

---

4 Reported in the Guardian Wednesday March 27, 2002

before the June 1998 incident. But since the assault by
the 14 year-old boy, identified only as D, she has suffered
severe psychiatric problems and taken early retirement.
Miss Waugh, 53, of Chigwell Row, Essex, was speaking
to the head teacher when D came in behind her, covered
her face with his hands and forced his nails in. She told
Mr Justice Cooke: "I was plunged into darkness and
felt terrible pain. It felt like my nose was being ripped
off and my eyes gouged out." Her minor facial injuries
healed but she developed severe post traumatic stress
disorder and still requires intensive therapy. D, who had
vision and mobility problems, was recorded as having
multiple handicaps at the age of three and was known to
lash out. Teachers were warned not to bend down near
him and told to hold his wrists if he was agitated or if
someone smaller went by. Miss Waugh's counsel, Simon
Dyer, said: "This child was known to be dangerous
and therefore reasonable steps should have been taken
by these defendants to ensure he did not attack Judith
Waugh, or indeed anybody else." The judge ruled that
the London borough of Newham, which denied liability,
was negligent in not telling the escort who brought D to
school of the need for a fuller restraint so he could not
break free."

Recent figures from the unions show teachers won an estimated £20m in compensation for accidents and injuries in 2006.

In January 2003 the Scottish Secondary Teachers' Association commented on the latest set of figures on violent incidents against teachers in Scotland's schools. The General Secretary David Eaglesham said:

"The continued rise in the number of violent incidents
against teachers and other staff in schools gives us great
cause for concern. Over 4 years, the number of reported

incidents has risen from under 2,000 to around 5,500, a rise of over 275 per cent. While a proportion of this can correctly be attributed to better and more accurate reporting of incidents by teachers, schools and local authorities, it is not acceptable to continue to say that the whole increase reflects a "bedding in" of statistics. The reality is that more and more of the extent of the problems of violence in schools is being revealed through these figures."

"The trend in the statistics on violence in schools correlates at a high level with reports of increased violence against colleagues in the health services, emergency services and other areas of public service. It is clear that society as a whole has become more aggressive in many ways, including road and air rage, and that schools are not exempt from this."

The main findings of the Scottish survey are:

- During 2001/02, the total number of incidents reported against local authority school staff (both teaching and non-teaching) was 5,412.

- 37 per cent of these incidents occurred within the primary sector, 30 per cent in the secondary sector, 32 per cent in the special sector and, two per cent in pre-school centres of education.

- Two thirds of the incidents reported involved teaching staff. There were 64 incidents against teaching staff per 1,000 teachers.

- 237 incidents (around four per cent of the total) were notified to the police.

- 98 per cent of incidents were recorded as occurring in school hours, with 50 per cent taking place in the classroom.

- 44 per cent of the incidents reported involved physical violence alone. 26 percent involved both physical violence and verbal abuse, and 29 per cent involved verbal abuse alone.

- In 94 per cent of all incidents reported, the perpetrator was a current pupil of the school. This is a rate of six incidents per 1,000 pupils. Where this information was available, 60 per cent of these incidents involved pupils with special educational needs (SEN).

- In four per cent of all incidents, the perpetrator was recorded as a parent.

On average there were five working days lost per 1,000 staff as a direct result of the incidents reported in 2001/02.

Children and Knives

Knives are now the most common method of killing people in the UK and knife crime in the UK is apparently reaching a terrifying scale. An exclusive study of statistics from 37 police forces reveals that 5,500 serious crimes involving knives were committed in just three months. That's one serious knife crime every 24 minutes. The figures include 55 knife-related murders, more than 2,000 stabbings and almost 2,500 knifepoint muggings.

To put this into perspective the Metropolitan Police recorded 1,580 offences across London between April and June 2006. It showed that 17 people are stabbed or robbed at knifepoint in the capital every day. The figures include 24 murders, 339 woundings and 1,134 street robberies. At the time of writing this book, a 17 year-old A-Level student, Rizwan Darbar, became the 21st teenager to be murdered in London this year.

In 2003 a MORI survey found that 29 per cent of secondary school children admitted they had carried a knife. That rose to 62 per cent among excluded pupils.

The recent MORI poll for the Youth Justice Board highlighted that a child dies from a knife attack **EVERY 2 WEEKS** in the UK.

The MORI survey also showed:

- Children as young as seven are carrying blades.

- The menace blights nearly every school.

- Two-thirds of stab victims never report attacks to the police.

- Fatal stabbings now outnumber gun deaths in the UK by three to one.

Other surveys reported in the press[5] in October 2004 stated that:

- One in six muggings involves a blade;

- 25 per cent of 11 to 16 year-olds arm themselves with knives;

- 28 per cent of boys and girls said they carried some sort of blade in the last year;

- 25 per cent of them had penknives and 9 per cent had flick-knives.

---

5 The Sunday Times, October 24, 2004 and the News of The World, October 17, 2004

- For children who had been expelled:
  - 46 per cent carried penknives
  - 30 per cent carried flick-knives.

- In a boys-only poll:
  - 42 per cent carried flick-knives in mainstream schools
  - 64 per cent carried flick-knives in special units.

Recent Cases

The high profile case of 10 year-old Damilola Taylor recently again brought home the severity of the harm that knives and other sharp implements cause in our society. One theory put forward was that the ten year old boy was stabbed in the leg with a piece of glass in what is colloquially known as 'jucking'[6] as he walked home from an after school computer class on November 27th 1999. He managed to drag himself 100 yards along the street before collapsing and dying alone in the stairwell of a block of council flats in Peckham, London.

Two weeks later, on the night of Friday December 15th, doctors were fighting to save the life of another young 13 year-old boy who was stabbed repeatedly in a suspected race attack in Littlehampton, West Sussex.

Other cases that have made the headlines are those of Stephen Lawrence, a black teenager from South-East London, who was stabbed to death in a racially motivated attack while waiting for a bus on the evening of 22 April 1993, and Philip Lawrence, the school headmaster, both killed by a single stab wound, the most common type of wound that causes death.

---

6 Derived from the Jamaican verb 'juck'— to chop, stab or poke

As we are writing this book, we are reminded of the recent death in London of Martin Dinnegan, a 14 year-old boy, who was killed with a knife. His stabbing was the seventh fatal stabbing of a teenager in London alone in a six-month period. He was stabbed half-a mile away from where I was working at the time.

A knife is a very deadly weapon. Statistically, it has been shown that 30 per cent of individuals stabbed will die from their wounds as opposed to 10 per cent of people who are shot, yet we treat the knife as a lesser weapon than a firearm. This risk is further compounded by the ridiculous techniques taught as 'defences against a knife' on certain breakaway and self-defence/personal protection courses. Such techniques are in the vast majority of cases useless and highly likely to fail. As such they are negligent and possibly even unlawful in terms of instruction given regarding the context in which they are taught.

Furthermore, new legislation has now allowed head teachers of schools, and other authorised staff, to stop, search and seize knives from children, and if necessary, use reasonable force to do so. More on that later on in the book.

The skill of responsible organisations and the ethos that should be promoted by responsible and competent management is to balance the risk posed to vulnerable children entrusted into their care, and the risk that the same vulnerable children may pose to the staff employed to care for them.

Chapter 2
Defining
Physical Restraint

Physical restraint, also referred to as physical intervention, can be defined as the positive application of force for the purpose of overcoming a person's resistance.

Generally, restraint differs from force used in self-defence, by way of its applied intention. For example, defensive force used to protect oneself from a serious and imminent assault will normally be a reactive response, whereas physical restraint, especially if used to fulfil the requirements of an employee's job description, can be considered a pro-active use of force option.

"Physical Restraint is holding a child to restrict their movement. In this guidance we refer to physical restraint as holding them to prevent harm."

Holding Safely, The Scottish Institute
for Residential Child Care, 2005

Restrictive and Non-restrictive Physical Intervention:

A restrictive physical intervention is a term normally associated with the actual use of physical force to control a person's behaviour and can be employed using bodily contact, mechanical devices or changes in the person's environment.[7]

---

7 Guidance on the Use of Restrictive Physical Interventions for Staff Working with Children and Adults who display Extreme Behaviour in Association with Learning Disability and /or Autistic Spectrum Disorders – Valuing People Document, DfES and DoH – July 2002.

A non-restrictive physical intervention is normally associated with a technique that does not use force against a person's will. As such the person is, to a degree, 'compliant' whereas if they were not, a restrictive degree of force would have to be applied against their will to achieve the same result. For example, assisting a person in walking or guiding a person by the placing of a hand on their arm or back would be an example of a non-restrictive physical intervention.

A child: The Children Act 1989 defines a person up to the age of 18 as being a child. Whilst children are able to make many decisions for themselves at younger ages, they are afforded protection under the Children Act up until the age of 18. It has also been recently acknowledged that the Children Act 1989 applies to those under eighteen, who are in custodial settings.

Restraint: The Department of Health defines restraint as being... "*the positive* application *of force with the intention of overpowering the child.*" By definition it is applied without the child's consent.

Holding: There are many situations when it may be necessary to hold a child. For example the Royal College of Nursing defines holding still as "*immobilisation, which may be by splinting or by using limited force. It may be a method of helping children, with their permission, to manage a painful procedure quickly and effectively. Holding is distinguished from restraint by the degree of force used and the intention.*"

Volume 4 of the regulations accompanying the Children Act 1989 also addresses one aspect of holding stating that it is "*a commonly used and often helpful containing experience for a distressed child*"

Escorting: "*Accompanying for the purposes of guidance or protection*": (Oxford English dictionary), this may or may not involve physical contact.

Physical Restraint, Health and Safety & Manual Handling

Physical restraint is an activity, which places staff (and others, including the subject being restrained) at risk by the very nature of its requirement. As all organisations have a duty of care to their staff under Section 2 of the Health and Safety at Work Act 1974, and a duty of care to others, including the person being restrained, under Section 3 of the Health and Safety at Work Act 1974, the activity must be risk assessed in line with the requirements of Management of Health and Safety at Work Regulations 1999, in order to comply with Sections 2 and 3 of the Health and Safety at Work etc Act 1974.

Furthermore, physical restraint is also an activity that requires staff to gain control of a subject by human effort, which in certain circumstances cannot be avoided. The activity therefore, and the training that is required must be treated as a 'manual handling' activity. Therefore, in addition to the risk assessment required under the Management of Health and Safety at Work Regulations 1999, employers, and professional consultants, must make a suitable and sufficient assessment of any hazardous manual handling operations that cannot be avoided in line with the Manual Handling Regulations 1992.

Within the Manual Handling Regulations a *"load"* is defined as any person and/or any animal, and *"manual handling operations"* means any transporting or supporting of a load (including the lifting, putting down, pushing, pulling, carrying or moving thereof) by hand or bodily force. The Regulations apply to the manual handling of loads, i.e. by human effort, as opposed to other forms of mechanical handling. Manual Handling includes both transporting a load and supporting a load in a static posture. The load may be moved or supported by the hands or any other part of the body, for example, the shoulder.

As you can clearly see from the definitions and inclusions above, physical restraint is a manual handling activity and must be assessed in accordance with the requirements of the Manual Handling Regulations and the Approved Guidance.

The Manual Handling Regulations and Associated Guidance establish a clear hierarchy of measures:

1. Avoid hazardous manual handling operations so far as is reasonably practicable.

2. Make a suitable and sufficient assessment of any hazardous manual handling operations that cannot be avoided.

3. Reduce the risk of injury from those operations so far as is reasonably practicable.

Individual Capability

The ability to carry out physical restraint safely will also vary between individuals. Sex, age, height, weight, health and fitness will all have an effect on the person's capacity for work.

The physical strength of women as a group is generally lesser than that of men. Therefore we need to be mindful of this when designing systems of physical restraint, particularly for females who may be expected to physically restrain male subjects.

Physical capacity also usually peaks in early to mid-twenties, declines gradually during forties and more rapidly during the fifties. It should, therefore, be remembered that the risk of injury from physical restraint is greater for staff in their teenage years and those in their fifties and sixties. Therefore, if mature staff are expected to physically restrain a child, we have the increased potential for injury to both parties.

Pregnancy has significant implications for the risk of injury when lifting and handling. Hormonal changes in the body will affect the ligaments, increasing the risk of sprain. In addition, there is the risk to the unborn child to consider. Therefore, physical restraint is an activity that pregnant women should never be expected to perform and care should be taken in the restraint of the same.

Obviously, existing musculoskeletal injuries will impede the capacity for work, as will other health problems, such as high blood pressure, heart and respiratory disorders. Therefore, if adult staff, who are possibly not in the best of physical health, are expected to physically control younger, fitter and more agile service users, these facts need to be factored into the assessment of risk with regard to not only the behavioural management plan for each child, but also with regard to the departmental strategy for the use of physical restraint (staff numbers etc.). It is also important to consider these issues in relation to how the actual physical skills are developed that will enable staff to physically control their client group effectively and appropriately.

Physical Restraint and The Characteristics of Skill Performance

When training staff in the use of physical restraint it is important that the techniques provided enable staff to achieve the desired outcome, i.e., the physical control of an individual with minimal risk to all concerned. Therefore, it is fundamentally important that the physical skills taught to staff complement their ability to achieve the desired effect.

Physical restraint, like any other physical activity, requires the use of various physical motor skills. Motor skills can be defined as movements that are performed with a desired goal in mind. In sporting environments this may mean achieving such aims as holding a handstand in gymnastics. In physical

31

restraint it means achieving the aim of staff being able to use each technique to an effective standard, in other words so that the technique works whilst minimizing the risk to all concerned.

To achieve this the staff expected to undertake the activity of physical restraint must have the ability to do the skill. The Management of Health & Safety at Work Regulations 1999- Regulation 13 (Capabilities and Training) makes this point quite clear as it states:

> *"Every employer shall, in entrusting tasks to his employees, take into account their capabilities as regards health and safety."*

The balance therefore in developing any system of physical restraint is aiming to improve the ability of staff through training whilst designing skills and techniques that they can actually achieve in real operational situations.

Ability

When we refer to ability, we draw reference to stable and enduring traits that for the most part, are genetically determined and as such underlie an individual's skilled performance. Abilities range from visual activity to body configuration (height, weight and build), numeric ability, reaction speed, manual dexterity, kinaesthetic sensitivity, etc.

However, there is also the difference in gender to consider that we touched on earlier in this chapter. This is an important factor to consider if the training is to be provided to a predominantly female workforce, for example, who are expected to physically control males. This is something we consistently raise in relation to staffing levels in many schools and care home settings where there are generally more female staff than male.

Recent research has highlighted some fundamental differences between men and women with regard to aspects of personal ability. Therefore, although men and women should be equal in terms of their rights of opportunity and the right to exercise their full potential, men and women are definitely not identical in their innate abilities. These fundamental differences, if not addressed in a competent training package, will only serve to increase the risk to all concerned.

For example, the Allied Dunbar National Fitness Survey found that men are taller and heavier than women and that men have more active muscle tissue and an increased blood volume than females, contributing to them being faster, stronger, more powerful and having greater endurance.

A summary of some of the findings from the survey are itemised below:

- Men and women have the same number of muscle fibres. However, the muscle fibres in men tend to be larger and this is thought to be linked to the male hormone testosterone. As a result men tend to be stronger and more powerful than women because they have a greater lean muscle mass.

- Men have 10 per cent larger hearts than women, therefore, having a greater capacity to pump more blood and oxygen around the body to feed the increased muscle mass.

- Men have 10 per cent larger lungs than women, resulting in a greater capacity to oxygenate the increased blood more effectively.

- Men also have 1-1.5 litres of blood more than women, and within the blood men have approximately 5.4 million blood cells per microlitre of blood whilst women have 4.8 million red blood cells per microlitre of blood.

This means that men have a greater capacity for carrying oxygen in their blood than their female counterparts.

- Women also carry 10 per cent more of their overall weight as fat than males. Therefore, the female heart has to work harder in order to deliver the same amount of oxygen to working muscles in a given time interval, resulting in men having more active muscle tissue than females contributing to them being faster, stronger, more powerful, having higher aerobic and anaerobic power and greater endurance, than the average female.

What this research shows is that the physical and physiological differences between the sexes means that men have disproportionate levels of strength, power and endurance than females do.

In the context of undertaking physical restraint this means that men will be able to rely on greater reserves of strength, power and endurance during a physical conflict situation. On that basis women who will be expected to use physical restraint will require more effective methods of control, especially if they are expected to control a male. Men, by contrast, should, generally, be able to use less force to achieve the same outcome.

Skill

To be skilled in the actual activity of physical restraint we must first define what we actually mean by "skill". To do this we need to turn to the definition of skill proposed by the psychologist E.R.Guthrie (1952), which captures three of the essential features of skilled behaviour. According to Guthrie, skill *"consists of the ability to bring about some end result with maximum certainty and minimum outlay of energy, or of time and energy."*

Individuals who are more proficient in achieving a particular movement goal usually demonstrate one or more of the following qualities mentioned in Guthrie's definition:

1. Maximum certainty,

2. Minimum energy expenditure, and

3. Minimum movement time.

Therefore, if we are to train individuals to be competent in the activity of effecting physical restraint in a competent manner, whilst reducing the risks associated with manual handling and positional asphyxiation, achieving these three proficiencies is paramount.

These fundamental principles are important factors to consider when designing the system of physical restraint and the techniques that staff will be expected to use. Therefore, we have covered the three qualities of "skill" as defined by Guthrie in more detail below.

1. Maximum Certainty of Goal Achievement

One quality of skill proficiency is movement certainty. To be *"skilled"* implies that a person is able to meet the performance goal, or *"end result"*, with *"maximum certainty"*. Only those individuals who can produce the desired result with a high degree of certainty, on demand, without luck playing a very large role, can be considered skilled or competent.

For example, it is no good teaching a skill or technique that individuals cannot readily apply competently in situations of high emotional arousal. If this is the case then the skill or technique being taught will have a high degree of failure.

This is a fundamental quality for all personnel expected to use physical restraint techniques. By the very nature of its use (if it is to be used lawfully) physical restraint should only ideally be used as a last resort and therefore, by default, is highly likely to be applied in situations of high emotional arousal where a degree of risk is ever apparent. If, in such situations, the staff members do not have confidence in their ability and/or the techniques they have been trained to use, for example they fear that the techniques they are trained in will not achieve the desired goal, these factors can lead to:

- Staff engaging prematurely to gain the advantage when dialogue and diversion would have been possibly more appropriate; and/or

- Staff not engaging when required to, for fear of being disciplined therefore allowing a greater harm to manifest itself to clients/service users;

When designing physical restraint techniques, it must be accepted that the goals that are to be achieved in training will be less achievable achievable in reality. This will be due to the added pressures involved when the member of staff is faced with the reality presented by a violent service user. For example, we need to understand as professional advisors or coaches that the goals, which may be achievable 70 per cent of the time in training, may only be achievable 40 per cent of the time in reality due to added pressures.[8]

This fact seemed to be proved in a 1997 in a Report by Her Majesty's Inspectorate of Constabulary regarding Officer Safety Training, which stated:

"A common complaint during the Inspection was that officer safety training, particularly in the use of certain batons, was overly complicated, requiring an excessive

---

8 Performance Profiling – The National Coaching Foundation.

*number of techniques... Most officers think they will
not be able to remember the various techniques in
confrontation situations and have forgotten them by the
time they attend refresher training. A study in one force has
disclosed that up to 80 per cent of officers assaulted during
the period did not make use of self-defence techniques
to defend themselves, despite being trained to do so."*

2. Minimum Energy Expenditure

A second quality of skill proficiency is the minimisation and
conservation of the energy required for the action. This means the
reduction or elimination of unwanted or unnecessary movement
which is crucial for those individuals who must conserve energy to
achieve success. This quality is an important goal for individuals
at the lower end of the skill spectrum, and for those who may
be required to use physical restraint in emotionally charged and
hostile situations.

If we apply this quality to the activity of physical restraint,
we can see the relationship. Many people who may be expected to
use physical restraint may not be motivated to use the skill. They
may have joined their respective organisations for caring or other
personal reasons and although they are probably (and hopefully)
competent and proficient in their professional abilities, they may
be at the lower end of the skills spectrum when it comes to the
activity of physical restraint. Therefore, it is imperative that in
developing physical restraint programmes for such individuals or
groups that we construct them in such a way so that they do not
require a high degree of physical or mental energy expenditure.

This quality also mirrors the legal issues on use of force and
it has particular bearing on the social policy on the minimisation
of force. Such a policy would promote the minimum use of force,
which although politically acceptable to many caring agencies, will
cause problems for those expected to use physical restraint skills.
This is because when attempting to comply with such a policy,

it allows a restraint to carry on for an extended period of time. If this occurs, staff will have to expend more energy to maintain or obtain control. This in turn increases the mental demands of the task, which increases fatigue, reduces the chance of achieving the restraint with maximum certainty and serves to increase the margin of error. This will lead ultimately to increased twisting and turning, increased pushing and pulling, and as such increased risk of injury to the staff executing the restraint together with an increased risk of injury (and indeed increased risk of fatality) to the person being restrained.

3. Minimum Movement Time

A third quality of skill proficiency is the reduced time in which the goal is achieved. However, if minimising time is achieved through speeding up a task by speeding up the movements within the task, then problems can occur. For example, a typist who speeds up the production of keystrokes on a computer may produce more errors in word processing.

This is an important factor to consider when designing physical restraint training programmes for operational use, including the techniques incorporated in them, as the amount of time that a restraint goes on for is an essential factor in reducing the risk to all concerned. As Nat Cary stated at a Police Complaints Authority Seminar in May 2000:

> *"The amount of time that restraint is applied is as important as the form of restraint and the position of the detainee. Prolonged restraint and prolonged struggling will result in exhaustion, possibly without subjective awareness of this, which can result in sudden death."*

Therefore, to eliminate the risk of death we need to reduce the amount of movement taking place during a restraint. For example, prolonged struggling can lead to an increased build up of sweat which can diminish the effectiveness of the holds staff have on the subject they are restraining thus reducing the amount of control they have in a restraint situation.

This is also important with regard to technique construction where a system is devised around a number of differing techniques, or techniques constructed from a number of multi-movements where staff, like the typist, have to speed up their movements to finish the technique. The reality is that any individual who attempts to speed up a technique comprised of a number of compounded movements to reduce the time factor is more likely to make errors and burn up more energy in the process.

Increased movement results in the increased risk of fatigue reducing the capacity for the member of staff to think effectively and function efficiently in such situations, particularly if a more agile subject is being attempted to be controlled by less able staff than them. This can lead to an increased risk of injury to staff and children.

An appropriate and effective restraint system, therefore, needs to incorporate large major motor skills movements comprising minimal construction within its technique syllabus and not compounded multi-move techniques requiring minor motor skills movements.

Should there be a requirement for systems of restraint to be delivered that require more techniques or movements, then consideration has to be given to the ability of staff to be able to achieve the skills within such a system, the amount of time spent on providing instruction to allow staff to become competent in use of the skills, and more regular refresher training to ensure that the skills are remembered.

Ageing and the Skeletal System

Bone is a living tissue and like the rest of the body suffers from degeneration. As we age, the amount of bone mass decreases and there is a change in the make-up of the bone, resulting in them becoming less elastic.

Intervertebral discs also undergo change as we age. In a young person the pulpy centre contains up to 85 per cent water, but as we get older a gradual dehydration takes place. This effectively weakens the disc and lowers the level of loading it can tolerate. In old age these changes manifest themselves in the form of height loss, hunched backs and greater susceptibility for hip fractures.

Therefore as a general rule of thumb, children will have more natural fitness and agility than older more mature staff. As such, consideration has to be given to the age of the people likely to be restrained balanced against the ages of those attempting to effect restraint. For example, if two or three forty-five year old members of staff are expected to restrain a fit and agile 15 year-old boy, we need to devise skills that reduce the risk by applying the three fundamental principles that make up the definition of skill as defined by Guthrie.

Summary

In summary be wary of buying in "off-the shelf" standardised packages that teach the same skills to everyone irrespective of age, gender, natural skill ability or lack thereof. These standardised packages come with a degree of failure built in by the very nature of the fact that they teach the same techniques to everyone. In short, such packages, by the nature of their design, will have not been assessed for the specific area of work and the specific abilities and capabilities of the staff and service user group, because no specific departmental risk assessment has possibly been carried out as required by law. That means that what is being taught possibly breaches Health and Safety legislation, and possibly even Human Rights legislation by failing to take pro-active positive steps to prevent the unnecessary loss of life.

Chapter 3
The Difference between Common & Statute Law

Some employers provide advice and guidance for their staff, usually in absence of any formal training, that they should use their *"common-sense"* (initiative) in situations that they are likely to experience as part of their employed role. In addition I have heard, as I am sure many of you have, of staff being advised by their employer that they can use their *"common law rights"* in making citizens arrests or in going to the defence of staff who are being assaulted. The problem is however, that little or no information is forthcoming on what exactly *"common law"* is, and what the difference is between a 'Statute Act of Parliament' and a 'Common Law Right'.

Statute Law is law enacted by a legislative body. It is a written law, an act of legislation that is constructed under constitutional authority, which is aimed at governing conduct within its scope. They are enacted to prescribe conduct, define crimes, create inferior government bodies, appropriate public monies, and in general promote the public welfare. Such 'Acts' are often based on recommendations either by The European Union, or by UK bodies such as Government Departments, Commissions of Enquiry and reform bodies like the Law Commission. The House of Commons and the House of Lords then debate the recommendations at length, before being submitted for Royal Assent. The Human Rights Act 1998 is one example of a Statute Act of Parliament, as is The Criminal Law Act 1967, The Children Act 1989 and The Mental Health Act 1983.

41

The primary aim of a Statute is to provide a general protection for society by laying down laws aimed at governing behaviour.

Common Law on the other hand is the law built from the decisions of the judges in the courts and is based on the doctrine of judicial precedents. Common Law is a legal system based on judge-made English law with case-law precedents deriving from the decisions of judges rather than Acts of Parliament. Common Law came into existence to afford any individual who is attacked, or indeed threatened with a serious attack, the legal liberty to prevent, repel or terminate the attack, in order to preserve and comply with an individual's common law right to safety. Common Law, therefore, is primarily concerned with the basic right to life and personal safety. This is an 'ancient right' afforded to individuals of England in days before organised policing and the carrying of weapons was commonplace.

An example of where statute and common law co-exist can be found in Section 3(1) of the Criminal Law Act 1967.

Section 3(1) of the Criminal Law Act 1967 states that:

"A person may use such force as is reasonable in the circumstances in preventing a crime or in effecting or assisting in the lawful arrest of offenders or suspected offenders or of persons unlawfully at large."

Therefore, the legal right for citizens of the UK to defend themselves and make arrests is contained within the defined wording of the Act. However, the statutory definition provides the rider that any force that a citizen may use must be *"reasonable"*, and this word is not further defined by the statute itself. Therefore to find out what *"reasonable"* means we need to look at previous case-law decisions made by judges in previous cases.

The Statute 'Act' therefore, provides the general rule, but the aspect of whether the force used was 'reasonable' or not (in this example) will depend on the judge's ruling on how a person has exerted their common law rights with regard to the application of force in the particular circumstances. Therefore, the common law has an integral place within how judges interpret statute, especially and particularly, with regard to the use of physical force.

In addition to the above, we also have to consider that today's modern society, which is relatively well-regulated and well-policed, should provide general protection—but it cannot guarantee protection all of the time. As such the Criminal Law (and other Statute Acts of Parliament) have to respect individual autonomy (the right of the individual to act independently—to self-govern themselves and their behaviour), when society cannot provide immediate protection.

As a result, every citizen of the United Kingdom has the right (based on individual autonomy) to defend themselves, their home, their family and their property, should they be exposed to an imminent or sudden attack. This becomes more predominant when protection by society (the Police for example) is less likely to be available, or when such provision is unlikely to be immediate or provided within a reasonable period of time.

How far can we actually go when using force?

So far we have looked at what Common Law means and we have compared it with what a Statute Act of Parliament is. We have also touched on 'individual autonomy'—the right of the individual to act independently—to self-govern themselves and their behaviour. This means that each individual is entitled to use their own personal judgement, based on their own personal skill level and knowledge available to them, when presented with a situation requiring their immediate attention, as opposed to having to 'weigh up the niceties of law' in situations of imminent threat.

However, how far are we actually allowed to go when using physical force, and to what degree does our legal right extend? This is an important question if we consider some of the risks that staff are being exposed to in some environments on a regular basis. This is also an important question when we consider the vulnerability of staff and/or service users with regard to a use of force situation.

The Common Law, and indeed the Criminal Law, is committed to ensuring that everyone's right to life is safeguarded and does not allow for the infliction of extreme force or harm to repel or defend against some minor infringement. The law only allows the person being attacked the right to use such force as is *'proportionate'* to the harm or mischief intended, or which they honestly believed to be intended. It does not afford the right to use a disproportionate or excessive amount of force to protect their right to safety, as that could result in the person being attacked being justified in seriously wounding or killing their aggressor, which may, in some circumstances, be grossly disproportionate to the harm intended by the assailant or criminal.

As such, we also have to consider the rights of the assailant. This is further enshrined by Article 2 of the Human Rights Act 1998, part 1, which states:

> *"Everyone's right to life shall be protected by law. No one shall be deprived of his life intentionally save in the execution of a sentence of a court following his conviction of a crime for which the penalty is provided by law."*

In essence therefore, the right to life is a basic human and civil right of all citizens that cannot be detracted from or discriminated against in any way.

What does this mean to me?

What this means is that all agencies must promote and take

pro-active steps to preserve the right to life where a risk to life is known. An example of this may be lone workers, who are expected to visit potentially violent service users. If there is a foreseeable risk to potential loss of life then the employer must take positive steps to eliminate or reduce the risk. This is consistent with the first part of Article 2.

In addition, any system of restraint imposed upon another by any agency must incorporate whatever steps necessary to eliminate or reduce the risk of death within its system of restraint. This would be consistent with the positive obligation to preserve life as required by Article 2(1) of the Human Rights Act 1998.

Ok, but what if I'm faced with a life-threatening situation without time to leave or to get the police to attend?

In the second part of Article 2 [Article 2(2)] it it implies that if we were to kill another, or cause death, even with intent, that it would not be in contravention of the right to life, provided it was *"absolutely necessary"* to do so. Article 2(2) of the Human Rights Act 1998 specifically states:

> *"Deprivation of life shall not be regarded as inflicted in contravention of this Article when it results from the use of force which is no more than absolutely necessary:*
>
> a) *in defence of any person from unlawful violence;*
>
> b) *in order to effect a lawful arrest or to prevent the escape of a person lawfully detained;*
>
> c) *in action lawfully taken for the purpose of quelling a riot or insurrection."*

This would seem to infer that an innocent person's rights are absolute when protecting oneself or defending one's property.

This is something the Common Law has accepted for some time, and elements of it still remain as part of our basic set of Common Law Rights.

The idea is that the aggressor forfeits their normal rights when they embark on an assault on a law-abiding person, and that it is the aggressors misconduct in starting the conflict, which justifies the law in giving preference to the liberty and rights of the victim over theirs.

Now this is not as objectionable as it would first seem. If faced with an aggressor armed with a knife for example we can begin to see how this might apply in context. But it should be noted that this in itself does not allow the person being attacked to stand fast and use whatever force they may choose to use. In short we can not use a sledgehammer to crack a nut, as this would not take into consideration, or acknowledge, the rights of the aggressor. Such circumstances could ultimately lead to a society free to be motivated by revenge and retribution as opposed to lawful justification.

This principle has particular relevance if the aggressor is a vulnerable service-user who may not have the full faculty of mental ability afforded to them, and as such their attack is not motivated by malice, but possibly as a by-product of their confused mental state compounded with frustration and personal distress.

So how far can we go?

Article 2 of the Human Rights Act 1998 declares that all people have the right to life and then lists three justifications for the use of force that may cause death. However, the wording in Part 2 of Article 2 namely *"absolutely necessary"* creates a stricter and more compelling test than that normally applied by *"reasonable force"*.

Article 2 suggests that the law in terms of what is *'reasonable'* is too loose, and has adopted the wording *"absolutely necessary"* and *"strictly proportionate"* to ensure that any use of force that may lead to the risk of death is *"strictly controlled"* by authorising agencies.

The adoption of *"strictly proportionate"* shows respect for the rights of the attacker in cases of self-defence. What is important is that it should rule out the infliction or risk of considerable physical harm merely to apprehend, for example, a fleeing thief, or to stop minor property loss or damage etc. As a 19th Century Royal Commission remarked: " *a law whose only requirement was necessity would justify every weak lad whose hair was about to be pulled by a stronger one, in shooting the bully if he could not otherwise prevent the assault."*

What does this mean to me?

In short, it means that you have the right to life and you can take life to preserve your life, if unlawful force is being used against you that is a threat to your life, and if it has become absolutely necessary to do so—in essence, there is no other lesser option available to you at that moment in time to prevent the loss of your life (or that of another).

What about vulnerable people?

Staff too may be vulnerable! Therefore, if there is a risk of death to staff or to a vulnerable person in their care, then the employer needs to ensure that the systems in place, be they systems of physical restraint, self-defence or other risk management systems, reduce as far as possible the risk of loss of life as a primary consideration. This may have implications in some work environments in terms of ensuring that there are adequate numbers of staff on duty, as well as ensuring that they are able and competent in carrying out the tasks associated with their employed role.

Summary

In summary, the right to life is an absolute right that all citizens of the UK are entitled to enjoy. That means that employers must look for foreseeable risks that may cause a loss of life and take whatever positive and pro-active steps necessary to eliminate or reduce the loss of life. This applies to staff as well as to those that staff look after.

With regard to the issue of physical restraint, all employers and commissioning agencies for training and training providers must employ techniques and strategies that eliminate or reduce the risk to loss of life. This means that if a technique can be used that will promote the positive obligation to preserve life it absolutely must be used.

This requires that all employers, care homes, agencies that commission training and training providers must ensure that the systems of restraint and breakaway they incorporate must comply with the Convention standard required by Human Rights legislation by promoting the positive obligation to preserve life as required by law.

However, if employers and other advising agencies are promoting that staff should use their 'common law' (or just their 'common sense'), particularly in lieu or absence of any formal training, they are actually authorising and encouraging their staff to use their individual autonomy when confronted with situations of impending risk whilst at work. If so, it would seem perverse for the same employer to then expose staff to internal disciplinary procedures or prosecution when that member of staff's actions are challenged, leaving them in the frame if injury or harm occurs to the person they used force upon. In short, the very employer who has tried to devolve their responsibility by authorising staff to use their 'common-law rights' then disciplines them for doing so.

In addition, such an omission could constitute a breach of a whole host of Health and Safety legislation, should injury, harm or indeed illness (e.g. psychological distress) arise as a result of inadequate planning, assessment, monitoring and control. Furthermore, if a death should occur, this could lead to a challenge under Human Rights Legislation, particularly where the death could have been prevented by the implementation of a strictly controlled training programme.

Chapter 4
The Children Act 1989

As we saw in Chapter 1, The Department of Health responded to the PINDOWN Report by commissioning the Utting Report (1991), which concluded that the implementation of the Children Act 1989 should prevent the likes of "Pindown" happening again.

The Children Act 1989 is the main piece of legislation in England and Wales that relates to the protection of children. Simply put, the Act sets out the criteria for making court orders, and the accompanying regulations set out how local authorities carry out their duties in respect of these orders or other obligations imposed under the Act.

Outside of Section 25 of the Children Act that deals with the issue of secure accommodation, there are no other provisions within the Act itself that relate to the use of restraint or the restriction of liberty in relation to Children who are not being looked after by local authorities, either in the authorities own homes or in homes provided by private companies or voluntary organisations.

However, the Children Act 1989 is the main piece of legislation in England and Wales relating to the protection of children, and Volume 4 of the accompanying regulations, which relates to residential care, outlines the circumstances when restraint may be appropriate.

It states in section 1.83 of volume 4 that:

> *"Physical restraint should be used rarely and only to prevent a child harming himself or others or from damaging property. Force should not be used for any other purpose, nor simply to secure compliance with staff instructions."*

The emphasis upon ensuring that children are not restrained simply because they won't do as they are told is re-enforced in the National Minimum Standards, Children's Homes Regulations 2001, issued under the Care Standards Act 2000 and which came into force in April 2002. The new standards add that:

> *"Physical restraint is only used to prevent likely injury to the child concerned or to others, or likely serious damage to property. Restraint is not used as a punishment, as a means to enforce compliance with staff instructions or in response to challenging behaviour which does not give rise to reasonable expectation of injury to someone or serious damage to property."*

In summary physical force should only be used on a child or young person to prevent actual imminent or foreseeably likely:

1. Harm to self;

2. Harm to others, and/or

3. Damage to property

It is clear, therefore, that the use of physical restraint purely to get children to do as they are told is not permissible. This raises questions as to what does one do when children and young people won't leave an office area or when they refuse to go to bed at a designated time. The Children Act regulations and the National Minimum Standards are clear that whatever the response, physical restraint should not be one of them and if it is, then staff are clearly leaving themselves open to allegations of inappropriate restraint. More appropriate responses may be by way of imposing sanctions, use of dialogue, distraction, etc and such alternatives will be dependent upon the age, level of maturity of the child and the particular set of circumstances.

A fundamental issue here is how potential '*harm*' is assessed and the likelihood of it occurring, as one should only use physical restraint to prevent '*harm*' to self, others or damage to property, (government guidance says serious damage to property). Section 1.83 of the regulations also states, "*physical restraint should be used rarely*".

Children's dignity should also be respected when considering which physical interventions are most appropriate. This is also addressed in Volume 4 of the Children Act Regulations, Section 1.83 states:

> "*Where children in homes have suffered particularly damaging experiences, and have difficultly developing the self-control or good personal relationships which diminish the need for physical restraint, it is important that sufficient, able staff are employed to ensure that the children are dealt with sensitively and with dignity.*"

With regard to "*children in homes who have suffered particularly damaging experiences,*" it should be born in mind that there is little dignity in children being taken to the floor and being restrained face down by staff. Such techniques were widely taught in the past and in spite of what is now known about the very real dangers associated with such methods of intervention, and in spite of clear guidance to the contrary, there are still staff who are under the impression that they are appropriate and preferred methods of restraining children. Thought also needs to be given to the potential for certain restraint positions to cause distress or "flashbacks" to children who may have experienced various forms of abuse.

In addition Section 1.83 states that *"it is important that sufficient, able staff are employed...".* Therefore, the employer has a duty to ensure that appropriate staffing levels are in place, and that staff are *"able"* (i.e., have the ability to do the skill to a competent level) so that if force has to be used on a child there are enough trained staff on duty to be able to handle the intervention competently, appropriately and effectively.

The Children Act 1989 and Restriction of Liberty

One of the most common questions we get asked on training courses is whether staff are legally entitled to stop a child leaving a care home where they believe that the child is likely to be exposed to a risk of significant harm. We regularly come across staff believing (or in some cases actually being told) that they are actually not allowed to act in the best interest of the child (or indeed other vulnerable persons), which in itself is contrary to the Welfare Principle promoted by the Children Act and the United Nations Convention on the Rights of the Child.

For example, we have known staff to be told that they are not physically allowed to stop a child who, by leaving a children's home, is placing themselves at risk of significant harm. We are also aware of staff having been told that if they are not trained then they are not allowed to use physical force, to intervene if a service user or member of staff is being assaulted or is about to be. Indeed some organisations actively promote 'no-restraint' policies to ensure that staff do not use force, and by doing so are then justified in their own eyes in not having to provide training.

So, let's say for example that we have a 15 year-old girl who is about to leave the home, and outside in a car is a man who is known to the authorities for dealing drugs and running prostitution rackets. The 15 year-old girl has a history or absconding and prostituting herself and the staff honestly believe that if they allow the girl to leave that she will end up either taking drugs or being prostituted by the man in the car. What should they do? Can the staff lock a door temporarily to prevent her from going whilst awaiting the arrival of other staff and/or the police, and can they, if they believe it is necessary to do so to prevent the child being exposed to the risk of harm, use reasonable force to physically restrain her to prevent her from leaving the home?

What is interesting when we pose the above question to staff and management is that most staff and management *believe* that they are not allowed to stop the child from leaving. This is even promoted by some inspectors of various regulatory agencies.

However, if we delve into the legislation we can see possibly where some of the confusion may arise. For example, Volume 4 of the Children Act Regulations states that states that:

> "...*it is important to recognise that any practice or measure that prevents a child from leaving a room or building of his own free will may be deemed by the Court to constitute "restriction of liberty". For example, while it is clear that the locking of a child in a room, or part of a building, to prevent him leaving voluntarily is caught by the statutory definition, other practices which place restrictions on freedom of mobility (for example, creating a human barrier) are not so clear cut. In the latter case, the views of the authority's legal department should be sought in the first instance as to the legality of the practice or measure. The views of the Social Services' Directorate might also be sought.*"

Interpretation of the above caused confusion for many in residential childcare. It was interpreted so literally by some, that agencies and staff felt powerless about preventing children from leaving children's homes, sometimes in the most worrying circumstances. The death of a girl in the care of Gloucester Social Services revealed the true extent of the confusion that prevailed in this area. Her file did not reveal any significant attempts to try and find out what had happened to her when she went "missing" and failed to return. A review of case records apparently indicated that at least fifty young people were missing from care homes in the area.

To clarify the situation further a Local Authority Circular [LAC(93)13] was issued on the 28th April 1993, under Section 7 of the Local Authority Social Services Act 1970 entitled *"Guidance on Permissible Forms of Control in Children's Residential Care".* It was disseminated to all Chief Executives of non-Metropolitan County Councils, London Borough Councils, the Common Council of the City of London, Council of the Isles of Scilly and all Directors of Social Services. The intention of the circular was to offer positive and practical advice to staff and managers on the care and control of young people in residential accommodation.

In addition, and very much aware of the confusion created by the misinterpretation of the Children Act, Sir Herbert Laming, the then Chief Inspector of Social Services Inspectorate, decided to address the situation via a letter of clarification entitled: *'The Control of Children in the Public Care: Interpretation of the Children Act 1989'* which he issued on the 20th February 1997. The purposeful intention of Sir Herbert Lamming's letter was to *"clarify further"* the Department's guidance in LAC(93)13 with regard to the Children Act 1989.

In his letter, *'The Control of Children in the Public Care: Interpretation of the Children Act 1989',* Sir Herbert Laming makes it clear what staff can and must do:

> *"9. The guidance in LAC(93) is clear that staff can and must intervene immediately to try to prevent young people leaving the children's home when there are grounds for believing that they are putting themselves or others at risk or are likely seriously to damage property."*

He then goes on to say that:

> *"10. Existing guidance [LAC(93)13 section 5] is clear that in certain circumstances physical restraint can and should be used. It is also reasonable to bolt a door temporarily to restrict a young persons' mobility, or in order to win some time to call for help from other staff."*

However, the use of locked doors should not be a substitute for lack of proper staffing levels and this if further clarified in LAC(93)13 which states:

> *"8.5 The use of locked doors should not be an easy means of saving staff time or to keep their numbers inappropriately low. Staff should be energetic in their efforts to find ways of keeping each child safe which minimises the need for physical control and restriction of liberty."*

Unfortunately, this extremely useful circular [LAC(93)13] and letter of clarification by Sir Herbert Laming, sent to all Directors of Social Services, does not seem to have filtered through to many staff working in this area. The experience of my colleagues and myself shows that once this document is brought to the attention of those working in the field, it is a valued document, providing useful and much needed interpretation and guidance.

The Children Act and Young Offender Institutions

In November 2002, the High Court ruled that the Children Act 1989 also applies to children in Young Offender Institutions and such children, therefore, have the same rights to have their welfare protected as others up to the age of eighteen.

Mr Justice Munby's decision was in response to a legal challenge brought by the Howard League for Penal Reform, who challenged the Home Office's insistence that Young Offender

Institutions were immune from the Children Act. The Howard League said that segregation and physical restraint inflicted under harsh regimes contributed to high levels of self-harm and suicide. (There were 554 cases of deliberate self-harm between April 2000 and November 2001 and 20 children have also committed suicide since 1990)[9]. Many campaigners have viewed the decision as a major development in terms of endorsing children's rights as well as an endorsement of the Human Rights Act.

According to the Howard League, young people in custody are routinely treated in ways, which would trigger child protection investigations in other settings. Listed amongst their concerns was the excessive use of painful restraint techniques. Justice Munby's decision could have an impact here. There is a need for staff to have knowledge of a hierarchy of physical skills, which should be taught within a clear legal context, and techniques that involve inflicting pain should not be used where a non-painful option can achieve the same result.

Techniques that have the potential to inflict pain, such as locks contained within Control and Restraint systems, are often very effective in securing compliance, and in some circumstances the use of such skills would be considered reasonable. Their use however, should be restricted to exceptional circumstances. If one gets into a position whereby policy states that such skills can never be used on under eighteens, then this would not reflect the broader interpretation of reasonable force nor the provision required by Article 2(1) of the Human Rights Act 1998. Moreover, such statements can effectively put other children at risk if we do not provide staff with effective methods of control. It is important to remember that bullying is rife in custodial settings and the main threat is from other young offenders. An inspection by Sir David Ramsbottom found that in one Young Offender Institution, all

9 Community Care Magazine November 21-27 and December 12-18 2002

remanded juveniles who had arrived in the previous ten days were in constant fear of assault by other children. If we remove from staff the skills that enable them to deal with the most extreme and violent forms of behaviour (when other methods will not suffice) we could effectively be removing their ability to adequately protect other vulnerable children and young people, and as such, it may be argued that they are not having their Human Rights upheld.

Government Guidance

Following the increase in concern about children in residential care during the early 1990's, the Government responded by commissioning a number of enquiries including the Utting Report in 1991 and the Warner report in 1992. The Utting Report concluded that the implementation of the Children Act 1989 would be sufficient to prevent the likes of Pindown happening again. The allegations continued, however, with enquiries into nursery schools in Newcastle, boarding schools in Northumberland and numerous children's homes in Merseyside, Cheshire and North Wales. In light of this, the Department of Health commissioned a further enquiry, Utting 1997, which also took into account children spending long periods of time in hospitals, boarding schools and foster care.

Some of the main messages included the need for increased vigilance, staff needing to be on the look out for potentially abusive practices, whistle-blowing procedures were established as part of good practice and improved vetting of staff needed to be introduced. The report also highlighted that effective measures needed to be in place to ensure greater safety for children.

In response to the exposure of this large-scale institutional abuse of children and young people, Government departments have issued extensive guidance aimed at promoting and protecting children's rights. Some of the guidance however has compounded the confusion that exists with regards to use of force and restriction of liberty in the childcare field. Jane Fortin, Lecturer in Law at

Kings College London, drew parallels with confusion that prevails in relation to parental powers to use force with children:

> "*The lack of clarity, particularly in the guidance to residential care workers, reflects the confused state of the law governing the scope of parents' powers to use physical restraint or force against children who are allegedly out of control. Unfortunately the current need for the law to conform with the requirements of the Convention has done little to improve the position since the Convention case law merely re-enforces existing doubts.*" (Fortin J. 2001)

An example of such confusion in terms of physical restraint can be seen in relation to the interpretation of the Department of Health document: *Guidance on Permissible Forms of Control in Children's Residential Care-LAC (93)13 Section 5.2* which states that:

> ... "*The proper use of physical restraint requires skill and judgement as well as knowledge of non-harmful methods of restraint.*"

Whilst of course physical restraint requires knowledge of the above, many trainers and those commissioning training appear to have interpreted this as implying that non-harmful methods of control must always be used. There will be occasions, however, when it is not appropriate to physically intervene at all, as the risk of injury will be too great, or perhaps a non-harmful method of control will not be effective.

Deborah Jones, co-author, wrote to the Department of Health in 2001 in relation to LAC(93)13, and received a helpful reply, which stated that:

> "*The guidance referred to above is intended to be helpful for those involved in residential care. It is intended to*

cover many of the circumstances in which it may be necessary to apply control. It was not intended to cover all situations and should not be applied without forethought"

Policy Support Officer, D.O.H.
(March 7th 2001)

Whilst not primary legislation, it should be noted that circulars and guidance from Government departments do have the force of law and breach of such guidance can result in successful civil actions. Having said this, such documents cannot cover every circumstance and eventuality, and they cannot over-ride primary legislation such as provisions contained in the Human Rights Act 1998 or our common law rights. These areas are covered in greater depth in Mark Dawes' earlier book, *Understanding Reasonable Force*. It is important therefore to try and seek clarification in relation to such guidance, as the consequences of misinterpretation can have profound implications.

Chapter 5
Educational Legislation

In Chapter 1 we looked at some of the risks that education and teaching staff are exposed to, including the risk of children carrying knives on school premises. Recent surveys and the high profile cases of those such as Philip Lawrence, the head teacher stabbed to death outside his school, highlight the seemingly increasing trend in the breakdown of good order, control and discipline in our schools, where many teaching and education staff feel that the children have more rights than they do. In addition, we read all too often of teachers being accused of assault by pupils, who then also face a long and protracted investigation into the allegation. The high profile case of Head teacher, Majorie Evans, highlights the problems that teachers falsely accused of assault face. She fought for 18 months to clear her name after it was falsely claimed she had slapped a child. It took two court cases, a further police enquiry, and then a school investigation before she was finally cleared of all charges.

The extent of the problem was highlighted in 2001 a BBC News article which stated:

> *"In the past decade, 1,300 teachers have faced allegations of assault—eight out of ten cases were found to have had no substance."*

Many, dragged through the mill by the investigative process and media, never return to teaching again. Some sadly even take their own lives.

However, school staff are legally required to safeguard the children in their care. At common law a teacher's duty is to take such care of the children in their charge as a careful parent would do *(Williams v Eady [1893] 10 TLR 41. CA.)*. The standard of care generally expected of a teacher is that of a reasonably prudent parent, judged not in the context of his own home, but in that of a school *(Lyes v Middlesex County Council [1962] 61 LGR 443 at 446)*.

It is also a statutory duty of every employee (including a teacher) whilst at work to take reasonable care for the health and safety of himself, and others who may be affected by his acts or omissions. It is also a statutory duty for the employer (school, Local Education Authority, etc.) to ensure the health and safety of its staff and others (Sections 2 and 3 of the Health and Safety at Work Act 1974).

In an attempt to help teachers promote the educational welfare of the students in their care, whilst maintaining good order and discipline, additional legislation has been introduced into the education sector over the past decade and this chapter gives an overview of some of these pieces of legislation that relate specifically to the educational sector.

The Education Act 1997 (Section 4 - Power to Restrain Pupils)

In terms of Primary educational legislation, one Act of Parliament which authorises staff to use physical restraint in schools, and the framework in which restraint can be used, is the Education Act 1997. Section 4 of the Act covers the *'Power to Restrain Pupils'* and provides the following:

4. (1) A member of the staff of a school may use, in relation to any pupil at the school, such force as is reasonable in the circumstances for the purpose of preventing the pupil from doing (or continuing to do) any of the following, namely:

(a) committing any offence,

(b) causing personal injury to, or damage to the property of, any person (including the pupil himself), or

(c) engaging in any behaviour prejudicial to the maintenance of good order and discipline at the school or among any of its pupils, whether that behaviour occurs during a teaching session or otherwise.

4. (2) Subsection (1) applies where a member of the staff of a school is:

(a) on the premises of the school, or

(b) elsewhere at a time when, as a member of its staff, he has lawful control or charge of the pupil concerned.

But it does not authorise anything to be done in relation to a pupil that constitutes the giving of corporal punishment.

Further clarification of what staff may and may not do when using physical intervention is given by Circular 10/98 which was issued by the DfEE to clarify what the Education Act 1996 provided (The forerunner to the 1997 Act).

Circular 10/98 states that:

21. Physical intervention can take several forms. It might involve staff:

- physically interposing between pupils

- blocking a pupil's path

- holding

- pushing

- pulling

- leading a pupil by the hand or arm

- shepherding a pupil away by placing a hand in the centre of the back or,

- (in extreme circumstances) using more restrictive holds

22. In exceptional circumstances, where there is an immediate risk of injury, a member of staff may need to take any necessary action that is consistent with the concept of reasonable force: for example to prevent a young pupil running off a pavement onto a busy road, or to prevent a pupil hitting someone, or throwing something

23. …In other circumstances staff should not act in a way that might reasonably be expected to cause injury, for example by:

- holding a pupil around the neck, or by the collar, or in any other way that might restrict the pupil's ability to breath;

- slapping, punching or kicking a pupil

- twisting or forcing limbs against a joint

- tripping up a pupil

- holding or pulling a pupil by the hair or ear

- holding a pupil face down on the ground

You will notice from the above guidance that more restrictive holds can be used in extreme circumstances. So can we plan for extreme situations? Well, the answer has to be yes. We have extreme weather warnings—don't we? Therefore, we can plan for managing extreme situations which may require the use of more restrictive methods of intervention, that is what a suitable and sufficient risk assessment is for.

In addition, the guidance also states that: "*In exceptional circumstances, where there is an immediate risk of injury, a member of staff may need to take any necessary action that is consistent with the concept of reasonable force...*" This means that staff can use reasonable force should they be confronted with a situation that they could not have foreseen. In short "*exceptional circumstances*" are situations that fall outside of the scope of the extremities of behaviour that had been assessed for risk.

Therefore, what the law requires is that employers plan for the extremes of behaviour which staff may be expected to manage and provide training that includes techniques that can manage such behaviour effectively, whilst also providing them with the judgement, skill and knowledge to be able to deal with situations that are exceptional, e.g., that cannot be planned for, by allowing staff the ability to use reasonable force. (For a full and in-depth explanation of reasonable force read our previous publication, *Understanding Reasonable Force*).

This section of the Education Act highlights that techniques that cause pain should not be used with pupils, unless the circumstances are exceptional and there is an immediate risk of injury. This is different than saying that techniques that may cause pain should never be used. More on this in Chapter 6.

Violent Crime Reduction Act 2006

The Violent Crime Reduction Act received Royal Assent on 8 November 2006 and makes provision for reducing and dealing with the abuse of alcohol, firearms, ammunition and also knives and other weapons.

What is of particular interest in relation to this book is Section 45: the power of members of staff to search school pupils for weapons. What this section does is basically amend Section 550A of the Education Act 1996 by inserting an additional section, 550AA, which authorises school staff to stop and search children at school when either the head teacher or a member of staff authorised by the same, has reasonable grounds for believing that the child has in their possession a knife or blade (contrary to section 139 of the Criminal Justice Act 1988) or an offensive weapon that falls within the meaning of the Prevention of Crime Act 1953. Such searches may be carried out on the school premises or anywhere else that a member of staff has lawful control or charge of pupils in their care.

Should a member of staff find a weapon, knife or blade they may seize and retain it, and, under part 8 of Section 45, the Act states that *"A person who exercises a power under this section may use such force as is reasonable in the circumstances for exercising that power"*.

Therefore, head teachers and staff nominated by the head teacher, may stop and search pupils for offensive weapons, knives and blades, seize the item and if necessary, use reasonable force to exercise that power.

Considering the risks posed by children armed with knives, blades and other forms of offensive weapons as discussed earlier, head teachers need to think holistically about how they will exercise these new powers when considering the foreseeable risk that teaching staff will be exposed to. This extends to ensuring that staff are appropriately trained and issued with the appropriate (and effective) personal protective equipment.

To put this into context, the general police response to a knife or an edged weapon situation is the deployment of a firearms unit. For example, in Preston in September 2006 a 15 year-old girl (who cannot be named for legal reasons) who was armed with a knife and making threats to kill, was shot by police with a stun gun.

Let us not lose sight of the death of Philip Lawrence, the school headmaster, 14 year-old Martin Dinnegan, 10 year-old Damilola Taylor and 18 year-old sixth form student Stephen Lawrence—all killed by a single stab wound.

The 2006 Education and Inspections Act

On the 1st April 2007, new powers came into force under the new 2006 Education and Inspections Act.

Under the new Act, teachers can use "reasonable force" to break up classroom fights when a pupil or teacher risks being injured, or to remove a pupil from the classroom. Teachers now have new powers to search pupils for weapons—without a need to call in the police. They are also able to discipline pupils who create trouble away from the classroom, outside school—for example on school buses or in shopping centres, if they see children behaving badly.

Previously, teachers had been allowed to restrain pupils under common law. However, as the common law was seen by many as 'vague' and therefore open to misinterpretation and misuse, the Government has seen fit to create yet another Act of Parliament to 'clarify explicitly' what teachers can and cannot do.

But will this create more of a problem than it will solve and has this been properly thought through? Has the need for the new Act of Parliament arisen out of a perception that teachers need more clarity on what their powers are—or could it have arisen because schools and their staff are not being trained properly in the first place?

Let us give you an example. Recently we were contacted by a school that required physical restraint training for approximately 100 teachers—in less than half-a-day! We were asked to work within such a tight timeframe because of all the other training requirements that the school was expected to implement on staff inset-days, therefore a half-day was all the time they had to spare.

In addition, the new Act places the onus and the responsibility to make the new statutory powers work, right at the feet of the Head Teacher of each school. This means that the Head Teacher will be held ultimately responsible also for any challenges, legal or otherwise, that may arise in the exercising of these new powers by school staff.

What Head Teachers need to be aware of, therefore, is where the common law was 'artfully vague,' this vagueness was, in many ways, it's actual strength. As Richard Card puts it in his textbook, *Criminal Law* (16th edition, 2004), and about which John Beaumont wrote in his article *The Use of Force—Reason for Optimism:*

> "The test of reasonable force might be thought to be so vague that a citizen acting in public or private defence has inadequate guidance on how far he may go. The vagueness of the test is, however, it's strength. It provides the flexibility to provide an appropriate response, however unexpected the situation, which a more detailed test specifying those situations in which one might use force would not."

Our concern for Head Teachers therefore, is that now that they have a new law, which is explicit in it's intention, they also now have a more rigid requirement to ensure that stricter controls are in line with other current statutory requirements. This includes compliance with Sections 2(2)(c) of the Health and Safety at Work etc Act 1974, and Regulations 5 and 13 of

The Management of Health and Safety at Work Regulations 1999.

Furthermore, as it is now 'reasonably foreseeable' that teaching staff are more likely to be expected to use force, as required by the new Act of Parliament, then training, it's application and the law associated with it, has to form a part of all teacher training if schools are to comply with the various laws and guidance associated with its use. This includes compliance with the Children Act 1989, the Human Rights Act 1998, Common Law and Criminal Law (Section 3(1) of the Criminal Law Act 1967), to name but a few. Failure to accept this and be proactive may lead to problems should an investigation arise.

Therefore, Head Teachers need to be mindful that these new powers do not remove or dilute the rights of the child enshrined in the Children Act 1989, The Human Rights Act 1998 and The United Nations Convention on the Rights of the Child.

Children have rights and all local authorities have a duty to actively promote these rights. As such all schools need to address in their risk assessments and behavioural management plans, those hazards or risks which are likely to be considered 'reasonably foreseeable' either as a causal or systematic result of how the new powers are exercised in each school. Indeed, this may need to be considered in relation to individual children, i.e. how the new powers may contribute to increased levels of self-harm or distress.

The new powers conferred by the 2006 Education and Inspections Act, therefore, need to be considered and applied very carefully. If not, risk of harm to both pupils and staff may be increased. Confusion or misinterpretation of the Act could also give rise to allegations of gross misconduct by staff and even referrals to the Protection of Children Act List.

This is most likely to occur where schools have failed to

69

implement proper training and guidance for their staff, resulting in staff having to revert back to using their 'common sense'. This was something David Leadbetter highlighted back in 1996:

> *"The historical tendency has been to individualise the management of challenging behaviour. To frame it simply as a matter of individual staff competence with risk viewed as simply "part of the job". This perspective has effectively de-emphasised the role and responsibility of the agency and focused the responsibility for risk assessment and intervention on the individual staff member, who inevitably remains in the frame when things go wrong."*

In short, if staff are not trained to a competent level, they should not then be blamed when things go wrong and they had to rely on their common sense, primarily because the school did not allocate enough time or resources to training them properly.

What Head Teachers must be aware of now is that this new Act places responsibility and accountability right at their feet. Therefore, any failure to train staff competently will leave the Head Teacher liable for any injury or fatality that may occur as a causal or systematic failure attributable to inappropriate training systems. We only have to look at the inquest into the death of Gareth Myatt, albeit in a custodial setting, to see the possible implications and consequences for Head Teachers, should a death result from a restraint attempted by inadequately trained staff, or from the fact that the system of restraint was not effectively monitored, audited and reviewed as part of the schools commitment to heath and safety. This could even lead now to charges of Corporate Manslaughter against the school/ head teacher.

If teachers are not trained to a competent standard, simply because not enough time is allocated for training to cover the foreseeable eventualities, this is likely to result in staff having to fall back and rely on their own 'common sense'. If so then the very purpose of the new Act, the need for further specific statutory clarification of a teacher's common law rights, has been compromised by the fact that staff would be reliant upon their common sense—which is why the common law existed in the first place!

The Personal Cost

The underlying principle that applies in relation to the use of force is that any force used needs to be reasonable in the particular set of circumstances. In the Daily Telegraph (November 29th 2001), the article titled *"Acquitted teacher sets precedent for force in classroom"* addresses a judge's ruling in which the judge endorsed the use of "physical force" by a teacher to restrain an unruly pupil. It is said that the decision is likely to have widespread implications.

The article states that a 64 year-old teacher *"restrained the 12 year old boy by putting him in an arm lock because he felt the child was about to cause a fight."*

During the trial, District Judge, Gareth Cowling, stated that:

> *"I have no doubt that the situation called for some authority and the use of some form of physical restraint and a teacher is required to use reasonable force. I have no hesitation in my judgement that in this case it was reasonable and Mr... is not guilty of assault."*

Whilst the relevant Unions welcomed the decision, it highlights how use of force with children and young people can be immensely stressful and how it can contribute to a culture whereby staff become extremely fearful of physical intervention. According to the Daily Telegraph , the teacher concerned said he would never set foot in a classroom again. The Chairman of the Governors at the school said that the teacher could still face a disciplinary hearing. Is it any wonder that schools are short of male teachers?

Although we need to have measures in place to protect children's rights, we need to balance these with the rights of other children to be protected, as well as those of staff. Often, the issue of techniques that cause pain is central to these arguments, since they are ethically more difficult to justify with children and young people. It is important, however, to be able to draw distinctions between legal and ethical issues.

It appears to us that a hierarchy of physical response options may, for many agencies, be the way to address the issue of teaching appropriate skills that comply with legislation. Emphasis should always be placed upon using those techniques that do not cause pain, with an acknowledgement that in exceptional circumstances; an intervention that does cause pain may be reasonable. In the latter case, where pain is used, it is our opinion that an assessment should always be made by a responsible manager as to whether the agency is satisfied that the intervention was acceptable. One of the implications of this would be that managers should therefore undergo appropriate training, looking not only at physical skills, but legal issues regarding the use of force, and at the dangers associated with particular forms of restraint. This would enable them to make more informed decisions and would go a long way to improving staff confidence and morale, whilst monitoring interventions to ensure that children are not being subjected to intentional inappropriate restraint. It also makes sound sense for managers to undergo such training as ultimately, they may well be held to account if things go wrong.

We will look further into the argument with regard to the use of more restrictive techniques, and whether or not pain-compliance techniques are legally excusable, in the next chapter.

Chapter 6

Does the Use of a Restrictive Technique that may cause Discomfort and/or Pain, amount to Torture?

"You never see a statue to a committee."

The King's New Clothes

Now there was once a King who was tasked with finding training, and one day, two *'accredited trainers'* came to sell the King what they said was training of a national standard.

The King was a wise and gentle man, and on seeing the various skills and techniques demonstrated, the King became very concerned. He was not sure that what he was being shown was appropriate for the welfare of his subjects on whom it might be used. Furthermore, he was also even more concerned about the complexity of the techniques and as such the ability of his staff to be able to use the system appropriately and effectively.

"Are these techniques suitable for what I require?" asked the King.

"These techniques are part of a Nationally Approved Course" replied the trainers. *"They have all been approved and it would not be wise for you to use anything other than what we can offer. You are aware of the National Standard promoted by the Department of Accreditation by Association, aren't you?"*

The King had never heard of such a Government Department. He also had no knowledge of what a good or bad technique would be since this wasn't his area of expertise. However, he was the King, and as such he believed he would be expected to know. Therefore, in an attempt not to look foolish the King said:

"Of course I have. I was just making sure that you were properly accredited."

Well, the truth of the matter is, there is no such thing as a National Standard, and the *Department of Accreditation by Association* was exactly what it said it was. It was merely a self-accrediting, self-regulating, organisation that developed and promoted it's own standards—nothing more. But the swindlers were very smart, and they said:

"Your Majesty, to a wise man this is 'approved, accredited and recognised training', but to a fool it is absolutely inappropriate and ineffective."

Naturally, the King not wanting to appear a fool, said:

"Isn't it grand! Isn't it fine! Look at the posture, the skill, the badge! The training is all together, but all together it's all together the most remarkable training that I have ever seen. These eyes of mine at once determine the skills as competent, the badge as lawful, I really, really must agree, I like what I have seen. Somebody send for the Queen."

Well, they sent for the Queen and quickly explained to her about the training. And naturally, the Queen not wanting to appear a fool, said:

"Well, isn't it oh! Isn't it good! Look at the way the instructors move! The approved training is all together, but all together it's all together the most

remarkable training that I have ever seen. These eyes of mine at once determine the skills as competent, the badge as lawful, I really, really must agree, I like what I have seen. Summon the Court to convene."

Well the court convened, and you never saw in your life as many people as were at that court. All the heads of department, the senior managers, the educational psychologists, social care inspectors, representatives from various other Court departments, and so on. It was just full with people, and they were all told about the Nationally Recognised Approved and Accredited Training. And after they were told they naturally didn't want to appear fools either so they said:

"Isn't it ohhh! Isn't it ahhh! Isn't it absolutely brill! The approved training is all together, but all together it's all together the most remarkable training that we have ever seen. These eyes of ours at once determine the skills as competent, the badge as lawful, I really, really must agree, we like what we have seen. Now quickly, put it all together with books with badges and letters so clever, train it in a way that no will ever question please."

Now back to the original story of the King's new clothes…

Now the day of the big parade came and the streets were just lined with thousands, and thousands, and thousands of people, and they all were cheering as the artillery came by, the infantry marched by, the cavalry galloped by. And everybody was cheering like mad, except one little boy. You see, he hadn't heard about the magic suit and didn't know what he was supposed to see. Well, as the King came by the little boy looked and, horrified, said,

"Look at the King! Look at the King! Look at the King, the King, the King! The King is in the all together But all together, the all together He's all together as naked as the

day that he was born. The King is in the all together But all together the all together It's all together the very least the King has ever worn."

Do you only see that which you believe you are supposed to see, or do you see only what you think others want you to see? If you do, are you very possibly leaving yourself extremely naked to the risk of an increased liability?

Remember: In the kingdom of the blind
the one-eyed man will always be king.

There has been a lot of debate in recent years regarding the use of restrictive interventions and pain-compliance techniques and quite a few myths and misconceptions have arisen. One being that the use of a pain-compliance technique amounts to an act of torture—especially if used on a vulnerable client/service user.

We have even heard speakers at events state that any technique that causes pain is a breach of Article 3 of the Human Rights Act 1998 since it would amount to an act of torture, especially if used on a vulnerable service user. This is even the view of some Government Inspectors—many not even trained in the legal aspects relating to the use of force.

BILD (The British Institute of Learning Disabilities), an agency committed to improving the quality of life for people with learning disabilites, is also opposed to the use of techniques that may cause pain, as the following extracts from various e-mails received from them illustrates:

"Morally and ethically BILD is opposed to the use of touching, guiding or holding techniques which might or are known to cause pain or discomfort, or techniques that are designed to use pain as an effective component to gain compliance and believes the presumption must be that they are not to be taught."

Furthermore, in correspondence received from QPM (the body that regulated CSCI) in September 2005 they make reference to Article 19 of the United Nations Convention on the Rights of the Child because they believe that Article 19 is relevant to the issue of *"pain-compliance"* as part of restraint. They also believe that any use of a restrictive or pain-compliance technique is tantamount to corporal punishment.

What Article 19 of the United Nations Convention on the Rights states is:

> *"Children shall be protected from all forms of physical or mental violence, injury or abuse, neglect or negligent treatment, maltreatment or exploitation, including sexual abuse, while in the care of their parents or of any other person. Child protection should include support for the child and their carers, prevention, identification, reporting, referral, investigation, treatment, judicial involvement, and follow up of instances of child maltreatment."*

In their e-mail to us, the QPM states:

> *"I make reference to the United Nations Convention because Article 19 is relevant to the issue of "pain-compliance" as part of restraint... I understand the term 'pain-compliance technique' to mean a method of restraint that uses the experience of pain by a child to bring about compliance. Such a method of restraint is unacceptable. It is a form of corporal punishment, which is contrary to Regulation 15(5)(a) of the Children's Homes Regulations 2001. The use of pain to manage children's behaviour could also fall within the ambit of child protection procedures... Consequently an inspector could legitimately say that "staff are not allowed to use pain-compliance techniques as part of a restraint of a young child."*

What is interesting about the final sentence of the above statement is that when we asked about an inspector's competence or qualification to make comments regarding the use of restraint, we received the following reply from QPM:

"Starting with your final question, inspectors observations about the use of restraint will be based on the regulations and standards and other relevant documents such as the United Nations Convention on the Rights of the Child. Whether or not an inspector has received training in the use of physical restraint, will depend very much on their own past experience and training. Such training is not part of the required training for inspectors."

In short, although QPM says an inspector *"...could legitimately say that staff are not allowed to use pain-compliance techniques as part of a restraint of a young child,"* the OPM does not state when an inspector might legitimately say this. Furthermore, they fail to acknowledge that there are also circumstances when such a statement might not be legitimately made, i.e. when the use of pain compliance might be considered reasonable in a particular set of circumstances. Nor do the aforementioned inspectors seem to have any formal qualification or competent training to make such statements. Whilst pain compliance techniques should never be used if there is a non-painful alternative, there may be exceptional circumstances when the use of such a technique may be the only way to avoid a more detrimental alternative.

If we read Article 19 of the United Nations Convention on the Rights of the Child, it does not specifically mention anything about restraint. Therefore, the perception of such inspectorate bodies and their staff, based on the comments you have seen above, appears to based upon their own subjective opinion of what they believe constitutes a breach of Article 19.

With regard to QPM's assertion that methods of restraint which rely on the use of pain to ensure compliance constitute *"a form of corporal punishment, which is contrary to Regulation 15(5)(a) of the Children's Homes Regulations 2001,"* this is not necessarily a correct legislative interpretation. Whilst any use of corporal punishment is contrary to the Children's Homes Regulations, restraint and punishment are very separate issues. Restraint should not be used to punish but only to prevent harm to self, others or to prevent damage to property, as stated in Volume 4 of the regulations accompanying the Children Act 1989. Therefore, if restraint is being used lawfully for the intended purpose of preventing harm, it cannot be defined as corporal punishment. The Children's Homes Regulations 2001 (which came into force on the 1st April 2002) state that with regard to Behaviour management, discipline and restraint 17.-(1):

> *"No measure of control, restraint or discipline which is excessive, unreasonable or contrary to paragraph (5) shall be used at any time on children accommodated in a children's home".*

Furthermore, the Regulations add;

> *"(6) Nothing in this regulation shall prohibit—*
>
> > *(b) the taking of any action immediately necessary to prevent injury to any person or serious damage to property";*

This leads us back to issues of reasonableness, excessive force, and the concepts of necessity and proportionality. These factors will depend on the particular circumstances of a given case. Two female members of staff trying to restrain a powerful 17 year-old male, for example, may well consider that the 'non-harmful' intervention they have been taught would be ineffective. You may say that in such circumstances staff simply should not engage. But what if they are faced with a situation of serious imminent danger, perhaps a younger more vulnerable child being attacked, or a colleague in danger? What if they thought they could engage effectively and gain control of the situation by using a technique which relied on pain compliance, and that by doing so, they could prevent a much greater harm from occurring?

Historically, by failing to acknowledge the limitations of some restraint methods, e.g. so called 'non-harmful' restraints, and effectively 'forbidding' the use of techniques which are often more effective, e.g. pain compliance techniques; it is our contention that we have perhaps unwittingly placed vulnerable individuals at even greater risk. In particular, when staff have resorted to prone position restraints as opposed to locks, thus increasing the risk of positional asphyxiation.

Perhaps in an attempt to address the moral and ethical issues that surround the use of pain with any individual, agencies have approved the use of other methods of restraint which may look more ethically sound, but are in reality potentially far more dangerous. Lack of knowledge about particular restraint techniques, together with incorrect assumptions and misinterpretation of the Law, contribute to the confusion that prevails in relation to physical restraint. This can result in staff working in a repressed atmosphere of fear of being disciplined, where the primary concern with regard to the use of restraint is not the welfare or best interests of the child (as required by law) but the best interest of the staff member themselves. By this I mean that as a result, staff are sometimes more likely to choose not to physically engage when perhaps they should, due to fear of disciplinary action and possibly even prosecution. Inspectors and managers sometimes fuel this by operating with a distorted perception of what they believe the law says about the use of certain restraint techniques. Such perceptions often appear to be based on their own interpretations of the law, which are often clearly wrong. Nor are such assumptions usually, in our experience, based upon a competent understanding of the skills and risks associated the real issues staff are expected to deal with.

We must stress that we are not promoting the use of pain over non-pain compliance techniques, where a non-pain compliance technique will achieve control. However, we are stressing that we must act in the best interests of the service user (as required by the welfare principle) and staff (as required by Health and Safety) in reducing any unnecessary risk of death (as required by the Human Rights Act) or serious injury. If this means that a pain-compliance technique is the most proportionate way of gaining control effectively and preventing a greater harm from occurring, especially where a non-pain compliance technique has, or is likely to fail, then yes—we are advocating that it should be used. Not only is this consistent with the law, but it is also morally and ethically correct if it is in the best interests of the service user and staff. Especially if it prevents greater harm from occurring.

The problem that arises is that by avoiding the use of pain compliance techniques, due to management or even inspectorate imposed sanctioning can, in some situations, increase the risk to the service user and staff. The operational contradiction that front line staff face as a direct result is: do they act in the best interests of the service user by using an effective technique that will protect the service user from harm, or do they use a ineffective technique that is likely to fail and act in their own best interest, attempting to avoid disciplinary action or criminal prosecution?

This seems to echo the words written by a man called Upton Sinclair over 100 years ago who said:

"It is difficult to get a man to understand something when his salary depends on him not understanding it."

Having said this, we want to stress that we are not advocating that pain compliance techniques such as locks should be used 'as a matter of course' with children and vulnerable adults. If such techniques are taught as primary methods of intervention, then this has the potential to create a climate open to abuse.

81

Agencies need to have systems in place to gatekeep and ensure that where a restraint involving pain is used, the circumstances are exceptional, e.g. involving serious and imminent danger.

But what if someone died as a result of an intervention not working properly (because the holds used were ineffective, or possibly even dangerous), and that death could have been prevented by the use of a more restrictive technique? Would that be a breach of Article 2 of the Human Rights Act? To understand this fully we need to know exactly what the Human Rights Act states.

Article 3 of the Human Rights Act 1998

When referring to "torture," we are referring to Article 3 of the Human Rights Act 1998, which states:

"No one shall be subjected to torture or to inhuman or degrading treatment or punishment."

Article 3 concerns itself with freedom from torture, inhumane and degrading treatment and punishment. The protections of Article 3 cannot be derogated (detracted) from in any circumstances, even during war or public emergency. For example prisoners of war cannot be tortured to obtain information because of the protection of Article 3. In short everyone is entitled to the protection of Article 3, regardless of their own conduct. Article 3 is provided to protect all individuals from physical and mental ill treatment and is relevant in a wide number of situations including detention, deportation or extradition, racial discrimination, corporal punishment and restraint.

The Government has positive obligations under Article 3 which mean that it is required to secure the rights guaranteed by it and to prevent breaches of the Article by one private individual against another, particularly against children and other vulnerable persons. As such there is a duty to investigate allegations of torture and to provide explanations for injuries—for example, where a prisoner or mental patient is found to have suffered physical injury.

To prove that torture has taken place, the evidence has to reach a minimum level of determination. This minimum level is relative and the criteria to prove that torture has occurred will possibly involve: the duration of the harm, its physical and mental effects and, in some circumstances, the sex, age and state of health of the victim.

There are no exceptions to Article 3, regardless of the conduct of a person and the State and all public authorities have a positive obligation to prevent torture from occurring. This 'positive obligation' includes taking proactive, positive steps by monitoring and reviewing practices and procedures, in line with current health and safety requirements.

Under Article 3, the State (including all public authorities) is responsible for the actions of its agents. Therefore, if torture, inhumane or degrading treatment or punishment is taking place the State (or public authority) will be accountable, not necessarily the member of staff directly.

Therefore, if restrictive interventions are being used regularly and pain is being unnecessarily caused, particularly where a lesser restrictive or less harmful technique could be as effective, then it may be considered that there are grounds for bringing an action against an employer for torture and/ or inhumane and degrading treatment and punishment. An example could be where a service user is being accommodated in an environment that does not have the resources to manage him or her, and as a result staff are consistently having to use high levels of intervention on a frequent basis to prevent harm.

Although based on current case law, a charge of torture in the above example may possibly be difficult to prove. Due to the high threshold of proof required, it may be possible to bring an action for inhumane and degrading treatment or punishment.

However, to put this issue into context, we also need to look at the first part of another Article—specifically Article 2 of the Human Rights Act.

Article 2 of the Human Rights Act 1998.

Article 2 raises specific issues with regard to the use of physical force in relation to the right to life. In the first part of Article 2, (which, like Article 3 is an 'Absolute Right' and so cannot be derogated against (detracted from), it states,

> *"Everyone's right to life shall be protected by law. No one shall be deprived of his life intentionally save in the execution of a sentence of a court following his conviction of a crime for which this penalty is provided by law."*

This statement is fundamental and important. It dictates that all State (or public) authorities must promote the positive obligation to preserve life. With regard to physical restraint, this has direct implications with regard to the techniques used. In short, if a technique can prevent the loss of lifelife, it must be used as this would be consistent with taking positive steps to preserve life.

The positive duty to preserve life is even more crucial when we consider those individuals who are vulnerable by nature, such as young children and the elderly, or those who may be more at risk of death during restraint, such as known drug users and people under the influence of alcohol, who may fatigue quicker after a violent struggle.

Risk of Death

One of the main causes of death due to physical restraint is positional asphyxia. This is when the position of the person being restrained, or the method of intervention, interferes with an individual's ability to breathe and they die from lack of oxygen. (More on this in Chapter 10).

A Home Office Police Research Group survey of 277 deaths in police custody, carried out over a six-year period, revealed a common factor in deaths linked to the use of restraint following a violent struggle. As a result the following recommendation was made:

> "*The amount of time that restraint is applied is as important as the form of restraint and the position of the detainee. Prolonged restraint and prolonged struggling will result in exhaustion, possibly without subjective awareness of this, which can result in sudden death.*"

Therefore, to minimise the risk of death, restraint should be used for the least possible amount of time. That means that the techniques used must be effective in terms of obtaining control quickly to bring the violent struggle to an end. This is especially important in technique design and development when consideration is given to the demographic make up of staff and the service user. In one care home we (NFPS Ltd.) audited, the average age of a member of staff was 42, and many were carrying injuries, including: ongoing back-problems, knee injuries, heart-conditions and wrist/hand injuries. This was in contrast to the service user demographic who were young people aged between 15-17, in good physical condition (fitter than the staff), had better natural physical ability and were carrying less injuries.

In the above example, staff who are expected to control a service user are already at a disadvantage. Therefore, any physical intervention programme needs to compensate for this by the inclusion of techniques that will allow the staff to gain control within a reasonably short period of time if the risk of serious injury and/or fatality is to be reduced to its lowest possible level (a health and safety requirement). It could be argued that failure to do so could result in a breach of Part 1 of Article 2 of the Human Rights Act—the positive obligation to promote the right to life by taking positive steps to reduce or eliminate the risk of death.

Therefore, if only non-harmful methods of control were available to staff, and this resulted in a restraint going on for an extended period of time, which resulted in fatigue/exhaustion that led to a death—the employer may have a potential law suit waiting for breaching Article 2 of the Human Rights Act.

If a more restrictive technique is used, however, possibly even a pain-compliance technique, then this could be consistent with the promotion of the positive obligation to preserve life as required by Human Rights legislation. If, however, the same outcome can be achieved by use of a non-harmful method of control, then that should always be the option. However, where a non-harmful method of control is highly likely to fail, or has failed, then the use of a more restrictive hold or the application of pain must be considered if that in itself prevents a greater harm from occurring.

With regard to the use of physical restraint techniques, therefore, all techniques must have as their primary consideration a design to minimise the overall loss of life. This is congruent with the positive obligation to preserve life required by Article 2.

An organisation, therefore, that promotes a 'minimal use of force policy', or even a no restraint policy, (more on that in Chapter 10) based purely or possibly on social, moral and ethical reasoning, could possibly be cited for a breach of a person's Human Rights should death occur that could have been prevented by the use of a more effective, including a more restrictive or even a pain-compliance, technique.

In addition policies and training that state that staff cannot use "pressure against joints" and "must not use pain" in the organisations 'approved' system of physical restraint, may actually be placing the vulnerable people at risk as well as their staff. These 'strict' and 'absolute' generalisations, albeit with good intentions, do not necessarily deal with the reality of situations in true context and as such are dangerous and can create liability.

If the misconception that underpins such policy is that the use of a more restrictive intervention (including the use of techniques that may cause discomfort and pain) is 'torturous' then the resultant outcome could be an increased risk factor for service user and staff.

The resultant paradox is that many staff, due to these sweeping generalisations, may be pressured into not acting in the best interests of their service user group—but instead, in their own best interests due to the fear of disciplinary action and the threat of prosecution.

The fact is this, if any force used is reasonable in the circumstances—it cannot be torture. The State would also have to go a very long way to prove torture, due to the high threshold of proof required. However, there may be circumstances in which, although the force used is reasonable, it may be possible to argue that the force used falls within the scope of degrading and inhumane treatment, and possibly even punishment. This could be argued if insufficient resources (including provision of adequate staffing levels) were in place, or if the service user was exposed to such treatment because they were in the wrong placement.

This, however, would be a charge against the employer—not the staff member. Especially if the staff were acting in the service users best interests, specifically where they were using force consistent with the requirement of Article 2—taking positive steps consistent with promoting the positive obligation to preserve life.

One point we would like to end on is one that is generally missed in these discussions. As you already now know, Article 3 of the Human Rights Act 1998 concerns itself with freedom from torture, inhumane and degrading treatment and punishment, and this is provided to protect all individuals from physical and mental ill treatment. This includes stress. What if the method of intervention used is causing staff high levels of distress because it does not work?

What if the distress that staff are experiencing is compounded by the fear of discipline or threat of prosecution because they believe that if they use a particular technique they will be guilty of torture? What if this fear is supported by incompetent advice imposed upon them by their employer or by a Regulatory body from a Government Department such as an inspector from the HSE or CSCI or Ofsted? What if the ineffective system of restraint used is resulting in high levels of physical injury to staff who are expected to take it because it is *"part of the job"*? And what if the continual exposure to the risk of injury, possible disciplinary action, and fear of prosecution are having a negative impact on a member of staff's mental condition? Wouldn't this also possibly fall within the scope of Article 3?

Beware false prophets – Monet and the King's New Clothes Phenomenon

Recently on an episode of the popular television series *Hustle* on BBC 1 which was a clever re-work of the fairy tale *'The King's new clothes'.* In the episode they managed to con a woman into believing that the clothes made of sacks were actually the work of an up-and-coming fashion designer, soon to be discovered. In an effort not to look stupid she bought into the story and was conned out of a considerable amount of money.

At the same time, the news was running an interesting story about Claude Monet, the father of Impressionist painting. According to many art experts, he is one of the greatest painters that ever lived and they accredited Monet with creating a new style of painting—Impressionism. As a result of Monet's new style of abstract painting and associated fame—many new artists were inspired to paint like him, some going to great lengths to distort what they really saw into a new reality that mimicked his style.

However, recently scientists believe they have discovered the secret behind the work of Claude Monet, and also fellow Impressionist, Edgar Degas. They both suffered from severe eye problems that affected their work. In short, Monet and Degas couldn't really judge what they were seeing—and what they were seeing probably appeared blurred to them. Hence, their paintings famous for their abstraction were actually nothing more than what they saw in reality, and not attempts to create a new, more abstract form of art.

With regard to the use of physical force, isn't it interesting how the subjective opinion of some self-regulated agencies and individuals, perceived as being experts, lends itself totally to acceptance by others who are conned into believing that they are right? In other words, they must know what they are talking about since they are the trainer, the agency promoted by a Government department—right? Not necessarily.

Now before we go any further, let us state that an 'expert' might not necessarily be what we think an expert should be. For example, a senior manager or an experienced member of staff can, in their own opinions, all be experts based on their own experiential perception of what they believe is true. This 'expertise' is then supported by staff who adopt the belief that they cannot do certain things and must do others because a 'expert' has told them so.

Recently, Mark was delivering a training course when one of the delegates raised a point which illustrates the above perfectly.

> *"Excuse me,"* he said, *"you are talking about the law, but you're not allowed to do that as only Judges are allowed to interpret the law."*

Interested by the comment Mark responded by saying *"that's very interesting, I didn't know that. How did you come by this information?"*

His response was as follows: *"Well I was on a course last week and that's what the instructor told me."*

"So does that means it's true?" Mark asked him. *"We'll I suppose so as he must know what he is talking about."*

Mark replied by explaining to the man that we all interpret the law every day. Every time we park our car, cross the road, purchase goods from a shop or defend ourselves or physically restrain someone we are interpreting the law, are we not? If only judges could do that we would all need our own personal judge, wouldn't we? The fact was until Mark re-addressed the issue, this intelligent thinking and functioning human being would have believed exactly what he was told, simply because the person who gave him the information, albeit wrong information, was viewed by him as someone whom he has placed in a default position of authority over him—because the person concerned was a trainer.

Another example which illustrates this, is advice given by restraint trainers. Some time ago John Steadman and Mark were being shown a particular holding technique from a syllabus that had been accredited by a particular agency. The technique involved approaching the subject from the front and then taking hold of the subject's left wrist with your left hand —a seemingly simple exercise. However, to execute this specific technique you had to rotate your left hand so your palm was facing upwards, take hold of the subject just above the wrist (from the front), then step around to the left hand side of the subject, pivot until you were alongside them and facing in the same direction and then complete the move by bringing their arm into what they called a 'figure of 4' position. However to execute the move from a person attempting it would have to put their body and hand in an unnatural position—which made the whole technique difficult to do. When we raised our concerns about this we were told:

"Well that's the way it's done".

"Do many people struggle with it?" we asked. "

Yes, but it has been devised by people who obviously know what they are talking about. Otherwise it would never have got accredited as an approved technique, would it?"

The above example appeared in our e-mail newsletter that we issue free each month and as a result we had an interesting e-mail from BILD (the British Institute of Learning Disabilities). The e-mail stated:

"Whilst I appreciate the article was a leader to encourage people to sign up for your Restraint Instructors Qualifying Course, I was concerned to note your description of the demonstration and subsequent explanation to yourself and John Steadman of a technique "from a syllabus that had been accredited by a particular agency." I presume you refer to BILD as the particular agency.

If so then you need to be aware that the BILD Physical Interventions Accreditation Scheme was designed and established to accredit the training organisation. It was not designed to accredit specific techniques precisely for the reasons you highlight. Part of the accreditation does involve commenting on techniques in relation to whether they comply with the guidance published in 2002 (specifically section 3.7). This is echoed in Section 3.4 of the BILD Code of Practice for the use of physical intervention.

Our intention following your article is to remind accredited organisations of this, but I would be grateful if you come across this type of misunderstanding in the future that you would refer people to BILD to clarify matters for them.

Many thanks
[Name and Title withheld]"

Deborah was once on a breakaway training course when she was being shown a technique to disengage from a front strangle. Realising the limitation of the technique she said to the course trainer:

"I've got concerns as to whether this technique would actually work if someone taller, heavier or stronger was really intent on strangling a smaller woman like me."
To which the course trainer replied *"Don't worry, if you are attacked, you will produce adrenaline that will increase your strength. That will make it work even against someone stronger than you."*

What the trainer failed to acknowledge was that possibly that the attacker would also be in a state of emotional arousal, whereby they might be producing adrenaline also, thus making them stronger as well.

Claude Monet, credited with being the father of Impressionist painting, was diagnosed with cataracts in 1912. He did not have surgery until 1923, and died three years later. He destroyed many paintings created when his vision was at its worst—even though he had painted them before he had his eye problems.

In essence, once Monet could really see what he had painted— painted he realised that what he had previously painted was not a true reflection of reality.

How many of us only see the distorted perception provided

for us by others? How many of us fail to question what we are being told because we believe that the person training us must know what they are talking about?

How many of us distort and delete the truth to make what is being imposed upon us work—and then carry the can when it fails? Or worse still, are blamed for *'not being able to do it properly'* when all the time it was actually what we were being taught that didn't work.

Chapter 7
Restraint v Abuse

The notion of restraint being a measure of control is itself controversial. For example, in the Waterhouse tribunal in North Wales, staff were criticised by Sir Ronald Waterhouse for using restraint as a method of control. He viewed the need for restraint not in terms of the need to gain (or regain) control of a situation or a person's behaviour, but as an expression of care.

As a result of the Waterhouse Report, along with guidance and legislation that promoted children's rights, authorities [including private companies] and their management, must protect children and young people from abuse when considering the use of physical restraint as a risk control measure.

However, a further controversial fact, whether we like it or not, is that in acting in the best interests of the child, physical intervention is sometimes necessary. In fact, if we fail to consider the use of appropriate and effective intervention, that omission itself could amount to an act of negligence should a child or young person become harmed as a result. This is especially true if the use of force would have prevented a greater harm from occurring.

Many staff today, however, are very concerned about false allegations being made against them should they use physical force with a child or young person. There is also considerable anxiety about the possibility of subsequent disciplinary action and/or prosecution that could result from such allegations. Furthermore, many staff worry about the potential to accidentally cause harm when physically intervening with children, as well as concern that in some cases restraint might be used inappropriately. The legacy of the Waterhouse inquiry, and many other inquiries into the abuse of children in the Care system, still cast a shadow over the issue of physical intervention with children and young people.

Physical intervention is normally applied without the consent of the child or young person. As a result it would be fair to assume that many young people who end up being restrained do not wish to be, and will, therefore, struggle against staff attempts to gain control of them, even though it may be in their best interests. This could lead to the child or young person perceiving the intervention as an act of 'control' rather than an 'expression of care.' This may then result in them portraying the intervention as unwarranted or unnecessary, making it more likely to be investigated as a potentially abusive act.

Even today, in the minds of many child protection social workers, there is no such thing as the reasonable use of force. Force per se is always unreasonable.

This chapter therefore has been driven by a desire to help front-line staff and their respective management address the issue of physical restraint, not only by considering the protection of the vulnerable service user, but also by considering the vulnerability and susceptibility of staff in some circumstances. For example when, in attempting to protect a service user from harm or prevent a service user from causing harm, they may end up being charged with abusive or harmful behaviour themselves, the implications of which can be personally and professionally devastating.

It should be acknowledged however, that abuse of children does take place, and some of those empowered with the responsibility of caring for children do breach their duty of care. History has shown us that it is all too easy for a climate of abuse to develop in organisations when misuse of power is not challenged and confronted. Monitoring and evaluating physical interventions is therefore crucial in trying to ensure that 'loop-holes' for abusive staff to hide behind do not exist.

The aim of this chapter is to investigate the relationship between the use of physical restraint as a risk control measure in promoting the safety and welfare of vulnerable service users and staff, and considering whether or not physical restraint is, by default, a form of abuse as some would have us believe.

Physical restraint by its very definition is force generally used without the consent or co-operation of the individual being restrained. In addition, as restraint is restrictive by nature, it carries with it a higher degree of risk than manual handling, which is normally undertaken in collaboration with a co-operative individual. Therefore, it is foreseeable that restraint generally promotes an increased risk of injury. As such, it is an activity that needs to be strictly controlled with more emphasis placed on alternative control measures and training, than an activity that has a lesser degree of risk.

We are also aware of instances of staff being investigated under internal disciplinary procedures for abusing children on the basis that they have caused significant harm to a child, when possibly they should not have been and it is the clarification of this issue that forms the basis for this chapter.

The reason why this issue needs clarification is that all staff in the child care sector have a duty to ensure that the child's welfare is the paramount consideration and at the forefront of their minds at all times. However, the conflict that some staff are presented with is that if they have to use physical force to prevent harm to a child or others, or serious damage to property, they are concerned that they could end up being charged with abuse or assault. In short the best interests of the child are, at times, overshadowed by the best interest of the staff member. As a direct result, many staff are more concerned with being investigated for abuse than doing what is reasonable to protect a child from harm.

An example of a recent situation we came across is as follows: A 15 year old boy was placed with a senior foster carer by a local authority Social Services Child and Family Placement team.

The child had behavioural problems, a history of violence and had previously had 18 placements in the previous 12 months. The child attempted to assault the foster carer's wife and was restrained by the husband by holding his biceps and sitting him in a chair. When the foster carer was visited by a member of the Social Services team the next day, the boy made an allegation of assault against the carer.

In line with local procedures, the child was removed from the carer's home and a case conference was set up involving Social Services and the police. With regard to the police investigation, no charges were brought as the police felt that the force used by the foster carer was reasonable in the circumstances in the prevention of an assault. However, Social Services continued to investigate the carer on the basis that he had caused significant harm to the child when restraining him, due to the bruising the child had sustained on his biceps.

The questions that should be asked here are:

1. What does the use of the words 'significant harm' mean, and in what context should the words be used? and

2. If reasonable force was used, could an individual still be investigated by a Social Services team for abuse and/or charged with an offence on the basis of causing significant harm?

3.   What are the implications of charging a member of staff with misconduct under guidance issued by Government Departments with regard to The Protection of Children Act 1999?

4.   Is it the individual who is solely accountable or is there a liability for the local authority?

1. What is the context for the use of the words 'Significant Harm'?

Significant harm is a term used as threshold criteria when investigating whether or not a child should be removed from home. The words *'significant harm'* are normally used when commencing care proceedings under section 47 of the Children Act 1989 and/or when applying for a court order [care order] to remove a child from its parents as defined under section 31 of the Children Act 1989.

Under section 31(2) of The Children Act 1989 *"A court may only make a care order or supervision order if it is satisfied*

(a)   that the child concerned is suffering, or is likely to suffer, significant harm; and;

(b)   that the harm, or likelihood of harm, is attributable to—

(i) the care given to the child, or likely to be given to him if the order were not made, not being what it would be reasonable to expect a parent to give him; or

(ii) the child's being beyond parental control."

For the purpose of clarification however, *'Significant Harm'* is not a criminal nor civil offence as no such charge exists. It

98

is simply a term used by social workers in proving that the abuse suffered by a child is both significant and harmful when considering the duty of a local authority in safeguarding children whom they believe to be at risk.

Therefore, the first issue to consider is that nobody can be charged with the crime of *'Significant Harm'* as no such charge exists in law.

What is 'Significant Harm'?

Significant harm is a threshold criteria used to prove abuse. To consider abuse therefore, one must first turn to its definition. An example of a definition of abuse can be found in the National Minimum Standards for Children's Care Home Regulations. In it abuse is defined as *"something that causes actual or likely significant harm to a child. It may be physical, emotional, sexual, or neglect of the child"*.

Significant harm encompasses two words, significant and harm (forgive us for stating the obvious, but we have good reason). The word 'significant' is not defined by statute, but the word 'harm' is, and we will come to this in a minute. When lawyers are looking for a meaning of something that is not defined by statute they turn to the rules of 'statutory interpretation'—in simple terms, they look up the meaning in dictionaries. Therefore, under the rules of statutory interpretation the definition of significant can be found as having, conveying a meaning, full of meaning, highly expressive or suggestive, important or notable (Oxford Dictionary). The definition of the word 'significant' implies that we have something which is either occurring on a frequent basis, or if it occurs once, is of quite substantial magnitude.

Harm on the other hand is defined by statute and specifically sections 31(9) and (10) of the Children Act 1989. Section 31(9) defines harm as meaning: *"ill treatment or the impairment of health and development."* Development means, *"physical, intellectual, emotional, social or behavioural developments, and ill treatment includes sexual abuse and forms of treatment that are not physical, including for example impairment suffered from seeing or hearing the ill treatment of another."* Harm is also further clarified in section 31(10) as: *"where the question of whether harm suffered by a child is significant turns on the child's health or development, his health shall be compared with that which could reasonably be expected of a similar child".*

So with regards to the definition of 'harm,' we not only have issues concerning ill treatment, including sexual abuse and other forms of ill treatment, which are not physical, but also concerns about the development of the child. 'Development' meaning the physical, intellectual, emotional and social aspects of the child welfare. In addition the child's development should be compared with that which could be reasonably expected of a child of similar age.

The interpretation of *'significant harm'* therefore, appears to indicate that 'significant' encompasses frequency and/or magnitude of harm and the implications of harm on the health, welfare and development of the child.

With regard to understanding the term *'significant harm,'* the following conclusions may be reached:

1. Significant harm is a term used as a threshold criteria when determining whether or not abuse is either taking place, or indeed likely to take place, when applying for a court order to remove a child from its parents.

2. However, if a child is placed into local authority care a member of local authority staff cannot primarily be charged with significant harm and/ or abuse simply because no such criminal charges exist. Outside of its use in care proceedings

100

(where the Court will determine whether there has been significant harm when considering an application by Social Services requesting a court order to remove a child from it's parents) the use of the term can become confusing and misleading.

3. Had the same injury occurred whilst the child had been in the care of his/her parents, it may have been argued that it constituted an abusive act. This might form part of an argument that the threshold criteria had been reached in terms of the parents having caused significant harm, and then submitted as part of the evidence required in care proceedings to obtain a court order.

4. This is not to say that an employee cannot cause harm that is by definition significant, but in relation to the issue of physical restraint of the child, the employee would, for example, be charged with assault or wounding if excessive force was used.

5. Therefore, if we are specifically talking about restraint then we do not need to talk about significant harm, but rather whether the force used was reasonable or excessive in the circumstances?

6. With regard to investigating restraint incidents (and indeed issues of self-defence), the term "significant harm" is redundant. It is best confined to care proceedings. To use the term outside of this context will lead to confusion and misunderstanding.

2. If reasonable force was used, could an individual still be investigated by a Social Services team for abuse on the basis of causing significant harm?

In the previous example at the beginning of this chapter (based on an actual incident) the social worker who said that the foster carer had caused *"significant harm"* appears to be the victim of muddled thinking. If the force used was reasonable in the circumstances (i.e. reasonable being defined as force being necessary, or honestly believed to be necessary, and in proportion to the harm prevented—then the foster carer, cannot be guilty of an offence, and certainly not one of significant harm as no such offence exists.

Although harm to the child may have been caused that was by definition 'significant,' if it is consistent with the wider interpretation of reasonable force and the positive obligation to preserve life as required by Human Rights Act 1998, then no crime would have been committed and, therefore, no charges should be brought.

Even if the foster carer hadn't used reasonable force, in other words the force was unnecessary, disproportionate and/or excessive in the circumstances, they still could not be charged with significant harm.

This is not to say that in the best interests of the child incidents involving the use of physical force should not be investigated. However, if those investigating the incident are unfamiliar with the concepts of law in this area and are basing their investigation (and possibly subsequent disciplinary action) primarily on the basis of abuse (based on the evidence that significant harm had been, or was likely to have been caused) and not on the concept of reasonable force and/or Human Rights legislation, then it is highly possible that the investigating officers will investigate the case from the wrong legal perspective. This could result in them wrongly disciplining a member of staff who may have acted lawfully and competently in the circumstances.

The implications of this can be devastating and can lead to a member of staff being wrongly prosecuted as someone who poses a risk to children or being wrongly referred to the Secretary of State for inclusion on the Protection of Children Act List 1999.

What does the Protection of Children Act 1999 provide and what are the implications of being charged with misconduct under guidance issued on the Protection of Children Act 1999?

The Protection of Children Act 1999 makes four principal changes to the Law[10]:

- It places the existing Department of Health Consultancy Service Index (a list of persons considered to be unsuitable to work with children) onto a statutory basis. It then provides for names to be referred to this newly created *Protection of Children Act List* and also a right of appeal to a new Tribunal against inclusion on the *Protection of Children Act List* (and also inclusion on *List 99*[11]. It also extends the scheme to health care services provided to children.

- It amends s218 of the Education Reform Act 1988 to enable the Department for Education and Employment to identify people who are put on *List 99* because they are not fit and proper persons to work with children.

10 The Protection of Children Act 1999 – A Practical Guide to the Act for all Organisations working with Children – Department of Health NHS Executive.

- It amends Part V of the Police Act 1997 to enable the Criminal Records Bureau, when established, to disclose information about people who are included on the *Protection of Children Act List* **or** *List 99* along with their criminal records. In this way the Act provides for a "one stop shop" system of checking persons seeking to work with children.

- It *requires* child care organisations proposing to employ someone in a child care position to ensure that individuals are checked through the "one stop shop" against the *Protection of Children Act List* and the relevant part of *List 99*[11] and not to employ anyone who is included on either list.

The Act also contains other provisions, the most important of which are:

- To enable organisations (other than child care organisations as defined within the Act) to refer names to the *Protection of Children Act List*;

- To permit the Secretary of State to consider the transfer of names currently held on the DH Consultancy Service Index to be transferred to the *Protection of Children Act List*; and

- To allow organisations to access the new *Protection of Children Act List* and *List 99* without first going through the Criminal Records Bureau until such

---

11 Information held under Section 142 of the Education Act 2002 (previously, but still widely referred to as, List 99) is a database maintained in the United Kingdom by the Department for Education and Skills (DfES). It contains details (such as names and dates of births) of teachers who are banned from working with children in an educational setting.

time as the "one stop shop" comes into operation within the Bureau.

If a situation arose and it was deemed appropriate to refer an individual to the Protection of Children Act List then the responsibility for this would rest with the employer. Additionally, for professional staff, the employer will also want to inform the relevant regulatory body of any action taken.

Misconduct from using "Intentional Inappropriate Restraint"

In a recent Department of Health document entitled: *"The Protection of Children Act 1999—A Practical guide to the Act for all Organisations Working with Children,"* reference is made to the use of physical restraint with regard to misconduct.

In section 7.6 (What constitutes "misconduct"?) the DOH document states that *"misconduct would range from serious sexual abuse through to physical abuse which may include intentional inappropriate restraint and/or poor child care practices in contravention of organisational codes of conduct which resulted in harm or risk of harm to children".*

Therefore, if a member of staff is disciplined for misconduct by their parent organisation for causing 'significant harm' to a child, and the result of that internal disciplinary is that the member of staff has been dismissed, removed from post and/or has left prior to the investigation concluding, their name may be passed to the Secretary of State for inclusion on the Protection of Children Act List as someone who is a risk to children.

However, if the employer is investigating staff who have used physical force to restrain a child on the basis that **'significant harm'** was caused, that would infer that the employer is investigating a use of force incident from the wrong legal perspective. The term "significant harm" is best confined to care proceedings, and issues involving the use of physical force to prevent harm must be investigated on the basis of reasonable force.

The implications of using these words out of context can have serious implications for individuals investigated on that basis, and found to have been guilty of misconduct.

What is possibly happening is that local authority child protection agencies may be comfortable with their understanding of the concept of 'significant harm', but are not comfortable with their understanding of reasonable force.

For example, a member of staff who uses physical force to stop a child harming themselves or others may cause a degree of harm to the child as no system of intervention can guarantee an unequivocal guarantee of safety. There are just too many variables are involved. However, if the force used was reasonable and not excessive in the circumstances, then no charges should be brought or proved if an allegation is made.

If, however, an allegation was made and an investigation was carried out by staff that are familiar with the term 'significant harm', but are not competent in understanding the complexities of reasonable force, the investigation will be flawed from the outset. In addition, if the individual being investigated (and/or their support agencies including unions, solicitors, health and safety professionals) are not aware of this, they may accept the internal disciplinary action by their organisational management, and indeed, even be advised to accept it by unwitting staff or union representatives. This could lead to an individual being found guilty of a charge of misconduct when they had actually acted reasonably and lawfully in the circumstances. As a result they could end up on a Protection of Children List when they have done nothing wrong.

To seek further clarification of this issue Mark wrote to the DOH and below is a copy of the e-mail sent and their reply.

From: Mark Dawes

Date: Friday, January 23, 2004 9:42am

To: info@dfes.gsi.gov.uk

Subject: The Protection of Children Act 1999

"Dear Sir/Madam

In your publication—"The Protection of Children Act 1999: A Practical guide to the Act for all Organisations Working with Children" you have made reference to the use of physical restraint.

"Specifically, in section 7.6 ("What constitutes misconduct?") the DOH states that "misconduct would range from serious sexual abuse through to physical abuse which may include intentional inappropriate restraint and/or poor child care practices in contravention of organisational codes of conduct which resulted in harm or risk of harm to children.

Physical restraint is an activity that carries with it a risk of harm to both children being restrained and also to staff who have to restrain children. Health and Safety Manual Handling research and research regarding the risk of fatality through positional asphyxia highlights that to minimise risk, restraint should be applied for the minimum possible time. This may mean that less able staff, i.e. those at the lower end of the skill spectrum, may have to use more restrictive holds to immobilise a child who is at risk to themselves and others, especially if that child is more fit and agile than the staff. This would be consistent with the positive obligation to preserve life as imposed by Article 2 of the Human Rights Act 1998 and must be in the best interests of the child.

However, my concern is that your guidance infers that staff can only use non-harmful methods of control and cannot use, even in exceptional circumstances, more restrictive holds and/or pain compliance techniques, even if such techniques were necessary to prevent a greater harm being caused. This is certainly the view of some trainers accredited by a particular organisation. As such staff may, by default, allow a child to be harmed in preference to using more restrictive holds and locks for fear of being charged with misconduct under The Protection of Children Act 1999 and subsequently being referred to the Secretary of State for consideration of inclusion on the Protection of Children Act List. Therefore, by default— decent staff will not act in the best interests of the child but in their own best interests ever fearful of being charged with abuse. There in lies the paradox of the predicament.

Being short and blunt on this issue, restraint skills are being taught that are based primarily on non-harmful methods of control with more restrictive locks and holds being excluded from the syllabus. As such these systems are limited in their effectiveness, are not being taught with the best interests of the child at the forefront of our minds, and are knowingly placing children at risk.

My questions are:

1. Where this is the case do such systems, that are knowingly being taught, constitute "intentional inappropriate restraint" for failing to protect children? And,

2. Does that in itself constitute misconduct?

It would clearly assist me and indeed many others if you would be so kind as to provide answers for me to the above questions to aid me in clarifying this issue further in consideration of the points I have raised above."

Yours Sincerely

Mark Dawes

From: [Name withheld]

Date: Thursday, January 29, 2004 5:15pm

To: dawes@markdawes.demon.co.uk

Subject: The Protection of Children Act 1999

"Dear Mr Dawes

Thank you for your emails of 30 December and 23 January. I am sorry for not replying sooner.

I note your concerns about restraint techniques involving children when applied to the Protection of Children Act List.

The extract you refer to from the POCA guidance is purely to illustrate some circumstances were a referral should be considered and made by an employer and is not exhaustive. If a referral were submitted to the POCA list when restraint had been used involving a child, this would have to be considered against the individual circumstances of the case and criteria for including a childcare worker on to the POCA list. In other words, the employer would have a requirement to show the restraint had harmed a child or placed a child at risk of harm based on the evidence made available. It is also important to remember the determination of any misconduct considered would be a matter for the employer to decide.

The Secretary of State would then need to be of the opinion that the employer had reasonably considered the individual to be guilty of misconduct that harmed or placed a child at risk of harm. In other words, if a referral involving restraint were made to the POCA list, the employer would need to demonstrate (for example), staff had received formal training and guidance on appropriate methods of restraint or that the restraint was not appropriate in the circumstances."

Regards

[Name withheld]
Protection of Children Act List Team

Department for Education & Skills

The above correspondence highlights a number of interesting points with regard to the use of physical force. Under the Protection of Children Act, it is the employer who is required to demonstrate that the employee was reasonably guilty of misconduct that harmed or placed a child at harm. In short, the employer would have to demonstrate that the restraint was not appropriate in the circumstances. In other terms, the use of force was not reasonable.

However, if the employer was relying on evidence from social workers, solely based on the aspect of 'significant harm' then the employer's referral could be based on flawed evidence and from the wrong legal perspective.

In our experience many local authority managers, including many front-line social workers, have little or no understanding of the concept of reasonable force nor of the complexities surrounding the activity of physical restraint and it's associated hazards. Therefore, no matter how well meaning their investigations are in this area, their judgements are likely to be misguided and based on evidential standards taken out of context.

In such circumstances, many professional social workers will be willing to give evidence (and can only be expected to do so) based on their own professional training and experience. In some cases it may be that when considering the best interests of the child as the primary concern, internal investigations may be flawed from the outset if child protection staff have to use their personal professional judgement as opposed to the facts of the case.

What this can lead to is an investigation based on the assumption of guilt as opposed to being objective and within the realms of natural justice.

Is there a liability for the organisation/local authority?

Obviously any individual responsible for the welfare of children in their care must act in the best interests of the child, and should have the welfare of the child at the forefront of their minds in all dealings with children, and be responsible and accountable for their own actions.

However, there is also a liability for the local authority or organisation in such circumstances. If a child has been placed in local authority care to protect the child from imminent or future abuse, then the local authority must be able to demonstrate and be responsible for the protection of the child from further abuse.

Historically if a child has been harmed whilst in care, it has always been the staff member who caused harm to the child who has been held accountable, and in many cases disciplined and/or prosecuted. An example of this is a member of staff who has used physical force to restrain a child and has ended up injuring the child by doing so.

In many cases, disciplinary action will be justified when considering the welfare of children, the history of children being abused in residential care, and the actions of staff in particular circumstances. However, the buck can no longer stop there.

The recent case of Lister v Hesley Hall sheds light on this perspective, and the case summary appears below.

Case Law – Lister v Hesley Hall[12]

"The recent House of Lords decision in Lister v Hesley Hall represents a major change in the law of vicarious liability. Previously, the well-established law stated that the more heinous the employee's act, the less likely it could be considered to be something for which the employer could be liable, on the grounds that it was less likely to be "in the course of employment". The Lister case seems to be a reversal of that view, and may have a great many ramifications, some of which are yet to be revealed.

This much can be gathered from the facts of the case, which consisted of a series of personal injury claims brought by former pupils of a school where they had been systematically abused by the housemaster (G). The claim was made against the school, on the grounds that the school was vicariously liable for the actions of G and, therefore, liable for the personal injury inflicted upon them. It was recognised by the House of Lords that G's actions were an abuse of the special position in which the school had placed him (to enable it to discharge its responsibilities).

---

12 As reported in Beachcroft Wansbroughs Employment Focus July 2001: Page 11, Issue 13.

Only by placing him in that position was G able to carry out the abuse, and he could not have done so had the school not placed him in a position of trust. The school was therefore, vicariously liable for those acts.

The Lords stressed that attention must be given to the close connection between the acts of the employee and the duties he is engaged to perform. In this case there is a close connection; there was a "care" element in G's duties and the way in which he discharged those duties were criminal. They also stressed, in perhaps the most worrying aspect of the decision, that a broad approachshould be adopted in considering the question of what falls within the scope of employment.

Whilst the decision is likely to have an immediate and substantial impact on those organisations responsible for the young and/or vulnerable—a wide grouping which includes not only schools but also nursing homes, colleges, prisons and old people's homes—the overall effects are likely to be more wide-ranging.

The Lords even suggested that vicarious liability might extend to occupiers of land in relation to their visitors.

A consideration of the reasoning behind the judgement suggests that an employer may be liable for any wrongful acts committed by an employee (for example breaches of the Human Rights Act, or if a manager sexually assaults a more junior employee) if it was the fact of his or her employment which provided the opportunity for the act to be committed.

It is too soon to tell just how far-reaching the Lister decision will be, but in the meantime employers should consider carefully whether their organisation could place employees in this kind of position, and identify (as far as possible) the best means of guarding against those risks."

The Lords decision in the above case stressed that attention must be given to the close connection between the acts of the employee and the duties he is engaged to perform.

Whilst employers may be vicariously liable, this does not necessarily exonerate staff nor mean they are not accountable or immune from prosecution for wrongdoing. However, what must be considered in light of new statute and case law precedents is that if a child is placed in local authority care the authority, in acting in the best interests of the child, must take pro-active measures. This means ensuring to ensure that all reasonably foreseeable risks are identified and controls are put in place to ensure the welfare and safety of a child previously identified as being at risk of abuse.

This also means ensuring that adequate staffing levels are in place and that staff receive competent training as is necessary to work in the best interests of the child. However, in many childcare settings, these control measures are challenged and compromised due to financial limitations that result in staffing levels being reduced and training being cancelled. When this occurs, front line staff responsible for the child's safety and welfare are put in the position of having to work with limited resources when it comes to dealing with more challenging behaviour. Yet, they are the very same staff who are likely to be placed in the frame when things go wrong due to lack of adequate resources and appropriate training not being in place. In short, staff are expected to undertake unsafe working practices to make an unsafe system of work function.

It cannot be acceptable to remove a child from its parents to safeguard them from abuse and in doing so expose him/her to a regime or environment where such risk is still apparent. For example, if a child has been removed by a court order having experienced physical abuse it would seem perverse that the same child could suffer similar or even greater injuries if placed in an environment where improper staffing levels and safe systems of work were not in place and where increased risk of injury is highly possible if restraint was used by untrained or poorly trained staff.

What must be made clear is that in such situations, liability also rests with the employer. When incidents occur that result in harm to a child, it should not only be the member of staff who is investigated, but the management process responsible for assessing and controlling the risk and providing suitable and sufficient control measures—including the provision of training —normally the first thing to go when budgets are challenged.

The real sting in the tail is the way in which local authorities have sometimes been known to interpret Section 47 of the 1989 Children Act. This section requires local authorities to make, or cause to be made, 'inquiries' if they consider it necessary to safeguard and promote the welfare of a child, providing they have reasonable cause to suspect that a child in their area is suffering from, or likely to suffer, significant harm.

This will be of no comfort to a member of staff who has been dismissed because the local authority argue that Section 47 gives them the right to make a child protection plan preventing a member of staff from working with children and dismissing him because of this. Two cases illustrate this point. In one instance the case was referred to POCA team and dismissed, but the staff member was subsequently sacked even though the same local authority disciplinary hearing concluded in his favour. In another case, a member was dismissed because he was believed to pose a risk, even though a Court had determined that the case was so unreliable that it was thrown out.

Any member of staff who engages in physical restraint is not only vulnerable to being falsely accused of harming a child (physically, sexually or emotionally), but is also vulnerable to being dismissed without any real safeguard. Members of staff need to be aware of these issues if they are to maintain their own health and safety at work.

Lillie and another v Newcastle City Council and others [2002] EWHC 1600

In 1990 in Newcastle, two nursery nurses were suspended for allegedly abusing children in their care. At their criminal trial the judge refused to permit the case to go before the jury because the evidence was flawed.

The local authority then set up a panel to investigate the allegations, chaired by an eminent professor of social work. Having determined that the two workers were guilty of systematic abuse the members of the enquiry panel, and the City Council which appointed them, were sued for libel by the two former workers. To win their case the claimants had to prove not just that the findings were wrong but that they had been reached through malice. They won their case and were each awarded the maximum sum available: £200,000.00.

Mr Justice Eady, the judge in the case, was scathing. He remarked:

> "One of the recurring features of this case has been the willingness of psychologists, professional or amateur, to impose pre-conceived stereotypes or theories upon the facts of the case. I have had to remind myself that evidence must always come first and theory kept in its proper place. It is obvious with the benefit of hindsight (and indeed should have been obvious at the time) that they were simply not equipped for the task. In any event, none of them apparently had any experience in conducting such an enquiry or in legal principles or processes (as to which, it emerges from their Report in several places that they were, in any event, quite disdainful)."

Two facts emerged with clarity. Professor [B] and his colleagues believed that the two Claimants were guilty of child abuse on a very extensive scale, as summarised in their Report, at the time it was published. I am equally satisfied that, despite their protestations, some of them had formed that view at the outset of their inquiry and never wavered.

It emerged early on in Professor [B]'s testimony that he has a fundamentally different attitude towards the weighing and analysis of evidence from that of a lawyer. At several points, it became apparent that he is rather dismissive of what he called "a forensic approach". He resorted from time to time to impressionistic mode, referring to his "professional judgement" and to discussions in academic and other published work. His colleagues were similarly minded. Indeed, Ms [I] [a member of the enquiry panel] voluntarily espoused the work "impressionistic". Yet the issue of whether any given individual has raped or assaulted a small child, or for that matter upwards of 60 small children, is not a matter of impression, theory, opinion or speculation. It should be a question of fact.

The Professor is entitled to be disparaging about the criminal justice system, or "forensic analysis", or the testing of evidence in cross examination. Many people are. Such criticism from the sidelines may or may not be made on an informed basis. But surely when such a critic steps forward to take on the responsibility of condemning a fellow citizen as being guilty of such wicked behaviour, a little humility may be thought appropriate. One would certainly expect a willingness to address the strength or weakness of the factual evidence relevant to the individual concerned."

117

As such, although their motivation was possibly correct in their perception, it was their ignorance of the process of law that led to their investigation into the allegations being flawed and as such, discriminatory with regard to the rights of staff and to the law of natural justice.

The following case highlights a successful appeal against the decision to be placed on the Protection of Children Act List. However, the case also throws up some interesting facts in relation to the issue of lack of training and no restraint policies.

Successful appeal against inclusion on the POCA List (Darren Mark Quallo v Secretary of State for Education and Skills [2003] 213.PC)

Mr Darren Mark Quallo successfully appealed under section 4(1)(a) of the Protection of Children Act 1999 against the decision by the Secretary of State for Education and Skills to include him on the POCA list, as an individual who is considered unsuitable to work with children.

The appeal arises out of two incidents at Tudor Lodge, a care home for children, on the 8th July 2002, as a result of which Mr Darren Mark Quallo was suspended from his child care post by his employer, Janine's Recruitment Team Ltd, and was referred to the Secretary of State for inclusion on the POCA list, which was provisionally approved by the Secretary of State on the 30th September 2002.

The appeal was heard on the 5th February 2004, Mr Darren Mark Quallo represented himself with the assistance of Mr A. Harris, operations manager of Janine's Recruitment Team Ltd, the Secretary of State was represented by Miss Karen Steyn of counsel. The counsel for the Secretary of State produced no oral evidence but relied on witness statements of two other members of staff, namely Sarai Burke and Iain Terry, incident reports compiled by each of them, and on records of reports made on the 9th July

2002 by other residents at Tudor Lodge, whom we will call: Child A, Child B, Child C and Child D. The latter (Child B, Child C and Child D) being the three complainants (plaintiffs).

The Tribunal heard the oral evidence of Mr Darren Mark Quallo, read his statement of the 24th August 2002, saw the video-taped interviews of Child C and Child D by D.C. Susan Lister and read the transcript of her interview with the appellant on the 29th August 2002.

The issue before the Tribunal can be summarised as follows: under section 4(3) of the Protection of Children Act the Tribunal must decide whether it is satisfied on the balance of probability that the appellant was guilty of misconduct which harmed a child or placed a child at risk of harm and that the appellant is unsuitable to work with children. If the Tribunal is not satisfied of both, the appeal must be allowed, otherwise it must be dismissed.

Tudor Lodge is a residential home in Purley, Surrey, for disturbed adolescents. Some young people are also educated there by teachers who come on site, and a minority of the residents go out to school. The three boys (Child B, Child C and Child D) who were involved in the two incidents on the 8th July 2002 were all being educated at Tudor Lodge.

The first incident involved Child C and Child D and, according to Mr Darren Mark Quallo, happened during the morning. The two boys, then respectively 14 and 12 years old, were playing with plasticine, rather too exuberantly; they were throwing it at each other and at Mr Darren Mark Quallo and took no notice when he asked them to stop. Mr Quallo then took hold of Child D's right arm and took the plasticine away from him. Child D was later found to have two bruises each the size of a 2p piece on his right arm.

The second incident was said to have occurred at about 6 or 7 p.m. on the 8th July. In this case Mr Quallo was watching the news on television when Child B, a 14 year-old resident, came in to the room, wanting to watch a boxing videotape he had brought with him. Mr Quallo told Child B that he could watch his videotape when the news had finished, but Child B was said to have immediately put his tape into the recorder. Mr Quallo removed the tape and returned to his chair which was by the door. Child B then opened the door banging it onto Mr Quallo's chair and Mr Quallo. When Mr Quallo got up, Child B went into the nearby piano room, where two social workers, Iain Terry and Sarai Burke were talking to Child C and Child D about the earlier incident. Child B apparently closed the door to the piano room behind him and would not admit Mr Quallo who was banging on the door demanding to be let in.

When Mr Quallo got in, a verbal altercation ensued and degenerated into physical contact. Mr Quallo seized Child B by his clothing and fearing violence (though much younger, Child B is about the same size as Mr Quallo), held him in a headlock. Urged by the social workers to release his grip, Mr Quallo did so, and Child B ran at him with a chair, so Mr Quallo again restrained him in a similar way, manoeuvring him into a prone position on a sofa. Iain Terry and Sarai Burke again prevailed upon Mr Quallo to release his hold and he did so, this time without further violence, and left the room. Child B was later found to have scratches on his neck and a bruise on his left ear lobe.

There are some differences in the accounts of those incidents. Child D, the 12 year old involved in the plasticine incident, said that Mr Quallo grabbed his arm and squeezed it really hard. He also said that Mr Quallo slapped his right leg and said that next time it would be his fist.

Child C, the 14 year old, said that having taken the plasticine from Child D, Mr Quallo came over to him, took his plasticine away and kicked him on his right leg, but did not cause any bruising. Child D also said that Mr Quallo kicked Child C's right leg and added that, at the end of the incident, Mr Quallo got hold of the back of the neck of his (Child D's) jumper, pulled him up by it and told him he should start to behave.

There were no adult witnesses to the plasticine incident, other than Mr Quallo, nor to the first part of the video incident. In his statement of complaint, Child B admitted inserting his videotape while Mr Quallo was watching the news. He said that Mr Quallo then kicked him out of the way and threatened him with his fist and used abusive language before removing the videotape. He said that he kicked the door causing it to hit Mr Quallo's chair as he left the room to go to the piano room. He did not mention barring Mr Quallo's way into the piano room but said that once Mr Quallo got in Mr Quallo grabbed him and held him against a window, while he, Child B, calmly asked to be released. He struggled and hit out at Mr Quallo who put him into a headlock, squeezing tightly so that he found it difficult to breathe. Eventually he managed to struggle free.

Child C and Child D did not describe the video incident in their statements of complaint, though both mention it, and Child C said he found it upsetting.

Child A (another resident at Tudor Loge) said that Mr Quallo pushed Child B against a window while holding him round his neck. Mr Quallo later put him in a headlock and squeezed tightly. Child A described Child B as extremely agitated and upset. Sarai Burke (one of the social workers) said in her witness statement that Mr Quallo had hold of Child B's clothing and was holding him at arms length away from him, asking for an apology. They were both shouting, Child B was asking to be released. She (Sarai Burke) and Iain Terry pleaded with Mr Quallo and Child B to calm down.

Sarai Burke also recalled two occasions when Child B threw a chair at Mr Quallo, but she was not sure of the sequence of events. In her incident report she also recalled the headlock and

Mr Quallo restraining Child B on the sofa. Iain Terry (the other social worker) said in his witness statement that he heard Child B laughing, then Child B came into the piano room and held the door against Mr Quallo who was trying to follow him. Iain Terry then told Child B, who was still laughing, to leave the door. He did so and Mr Quallo came in. There was some shouting and Mr Quallo grabbed Child B's clothing. Iain Terry tried to get Mr Quallo to let go. Child B tried to hit Mr Quallo, then threw a chair at him. In response, Mr Quallo got Child B in a headlock, holding him down on a sofa. Both social workers tried to get Mr Quallo to loosen his grip, but when he did so, Child B got another chair so Mr Quallo got hold of him again. In the end Mr Quallo let go and left the room. Iain Terry's incident report seems to support this.

For different reasons, the Tribunal was cautious about all of that evidence. A report by a consultant psychiatrist described Child B as one who has been observed to make up stories. Child C and Child D in their video interviews both indicated Child D's left arm as the one which the appellant held, whereas it was in reality his right arm.

It is plain that Tudor Lodge offers a home to some very disturbed children, who can be very difficult to manage. The medical reports and other documents about the three boys involved in these incidents made it clear that they all exhibit challenging behaviour, perhaps none more so than Child B, who was described in a psychiatric report as having "longstanding behavioural problems", being "physically aggressive towards staff", "deliberately antagonising" his peers and generally manipulative.

The Doctor who wrote the psychiatric report said that it had become increasingly difficult to set limits and boundaries for Child B because of concerns that this would result in either assault or self-harm. It was also apparent that Mr Quallo had very little training in dealing with these difficult children and what little he had, was by way of friendly informal advice from colleagues rather than any actual instruction. Moreover he had never seen a care plan for Child B though he imagined that there must have been one; he implied that, as agency staff, he would not see such things. The evidence gave the Tribunal the impression that agency staff, even of the appellant's length of service at Tudor Lodge, were regarded as temporary and were not seen as full members of the caring team.

The Tribunal was unable to find much to criticise in Mr Quallo's handling of the plasticine incident, it was not satisfied on the balance of probabilities that he kicked Child C though he did shout at both boys and grabbed Child D's right arm while he took away the plasticine. The Tribunal was not satisfied that he slapped Child D or made any threat to punch him with his fist. There was harm to Child D in the form of the two small bruises on his arm, but it was minimal. At the end of the video interview Child D said that he was not really upset by the incident and that it was not normal behaviour for Mr Quallo. The Tribunal agreed with Mr Quallo's comment that if the video incident had not happened, then the plasticine incident would not have achieved the prominence it did.

As for the video incident, the Tribunal found that it began with an example of Child B's antagonistic and provocative behaviour in taking over the television to watch his video while Mr Quallo was watching the news. As such Mr Quallo was not to be criticised for objecting and removing the video tape. Child B continued by banging the door, either once or more than once, into Mr Quallo's chair and then went into the piano room. In the Tribunal's view Mr Quallo is to be criticised for following him. Child B was obviously in a temper, there were two other staff members in the piano room and it would have been much more sensible to let them deal with him. By following, Mr. Quallo could only make the situation worse. His pursuit of an apology was ill-advised. To his credit (opinion of the Tribunal), he eventually heeded his colleagues' advice to release Child B and the incident ended. Mr Quallo should have brought it to an end much earlier by not going into the piano room; it would have been wiser to leave Child B to calm down and deal with him later. Mr Quallo admitted that he could have handled things better, and said that he would deal with such a situation differently, should it arise in the future.

The Tribunal found that Mr Quallo's pursuit of Child B into the piano room amounted to misconduct, but it was not satisfied that holding Child D's arm in the circumstances amounted to misconduct. Although there was evidence of harm to Child B in the form of a small bruise to his left ear lobe, the Tribunal was not satisfied that the scratches to his neck were caused in the video incident, and there was no evidence of anything likely to have caused a scratch. According to the doctor's sketch the scratches were almost vertical whereas scratches caused by grasping someone's neck would perhaps be more likely to be horizontal. Child B's medical records disclosed unrelated scratches less than a month earlier, on the 12th June. However, a bruised ear lobe is harm, if only minimal harm, so technically, at least, the Tribunal pronounced itself satisfied under section 4(3)(a) of the Act. The Tribunal did not find that any of the children involved in either incident was at risk of any significant physical harm beyond that which actually occurred.

Is Mr Quallo's unsuitable to work with children? He has been a residential social worker for some eight years, working with children for the last four or five years. Not only has there been no previous complaint about him, he had been working at Tudor Lodge, albeit as agency staff, for quite a long time and had been offered a full-time post there, which suggests a measure of approval. He was assisted in his appeal by the Operations Manager of Janine's Recruitment Ltd, his employer at the time, which can possibly be seen as an indication of the company's view of Mr Quallo. Child D said in his video interview that he generally got on well with Deon (Mr Quallo) and that the two incidents were not typical.

Mr Quallo's difficulty in dealing with the situation was compounded by a total lack of any formal training or instruction. It is both surprising and alarming that he had never been shown care plans, behavioural programmes or the like, to indicate in relation to each resident what the carers had to deal with and how they should manage difficult situations.

The social workers, Sarai Burke in particular, evidently told Mr Quallo about Tudor Lodge's "no restraint" policy when the incident with Child B was in its later stages. It was not wholly clear to the Tribunal, and was obviously not clear to Mr Quallo precisely what a "no restraint" policy entails, since restraint may be necessary and unavoidable, for example, where serious danger to staff or residents is likely.

Whatever that policy is, or was, it should have been explained to Mr Quallo when he took up his duties at Tudor Lodge; such instruction as he was given, (it seems to have been exiguous in the extreme), was totally inadequate. In those circumstances, the fact that Mr Quallo's performance fell below par on one particular day does not, in the view of the Tribunal make him unsuitable to work with children.

The Tribunal was not satisfied under section 4(3)(b) of the Act, accordingly Mr Quallo's appeal must be allowed. The findings of the Tribunal are in every instance unanimous; the Tribunal accordingly directed that the name of the appellant Darren Mark Quallo (also known as Deon Quallo) be removed forthwith from the list of individuals, kept by the Secretary of State under section 1 of the Act, who are considered unsuitable to work with children.

Chapter 8
The Myth that is
'Minimum Force'

Mark was recently invited to give a presentation at a Seminar event for an Association of Health & Safety Professionals on the use of *'Reasonable Force'*. Prior to his slot an HSE inspector gave a talk on the subject of violence at work. In his speech, he stated that as part of an HSE Inspection, Inspectors would look to ensure that only *'minimum force'* was being used by staff, who may have to control a service user.

Following on from that event, Mark was privileged to be invited to run a training event on the subject of physical force for a different organisation in a different part of the country. Whilst talking to many of the staff who were arriving prior to the event starting, Mark was informed that they had been advised that they *"were only allowed to use only 'minimum force' as that was what was legally required by the Children Act 1989"*. This was apparently the advice and guidance given to them by a physical restraint instructor.

Now these staff, including the HSE inspector, are good people. They do a difficult job, at best with limited resources, and in many cases, are left to use their own initiative in the absence of adequate guidance andw ith incorrect and/or inaccurate instruction. In addition, these good people, like many of you reading this book, are all primarily focused on reducing the risk of harm to the service users in their care, and also to themselves and their colleagues. This is possibly where the drive behind the use of the terminology *'minimum force'* comes from. However, what if the intention was right, but the application of the principle behind the intention was wrong, and this resulted in an increase in the risk of harm? If this is the case we have a paradox, in so much as the terminology designed to reduce risk is actually creating it. This is the basis for this chapter. we believe that the whole aspect of the use of the term *'minimum force'* is based, in the main, on a flawed understanding of the law in relation to the use of reasonable force.

This chapter is intended to clear up misconceptions regarding the use of the words *'minimum force'* and it's possible consequences. It also aims to address the conception of this term in context, whilst considering how it's application out of context can increase risk as opposed to reducing it.

Our concern is that the use of these words creates more problems than they are designed to prevent. For example:

- Government Departments issue guidance stating that only *'minimum force'* can and should be used.

- Local policies are written by local management that promote only the use of *'minimum force'* to control vulnerable service users.

- Staff are told by employers and training providers that because their service users are vulnerable, they are only allowed to use *'minimum force'*.

- Some physical skills providers develop and deliver training courses that promote only the use of *'minimum force'*, which are by design, limited in effectiveness. By failing to provide staff with the specific skills to enable them to adequately physically control some service users and/or provide protection to themselves, this can leave the organisation open to claims of negligence. For example, a teacher who was attacked by a dangerous teenage pupil at a special school won £190,000 damages in the High Court in 2002. The judge in this case ruled that the London Borough of Newham, which denied liability, was negligent for not revealing the need for fuller restraint of the pupil.

- Where an ineffective and complicated technique subsequently fails to prevent harm occurring to a service user, a member of staff may then be (wrongly) put in the frame for not being able to execute the complex physical skill effectively.

- In contrast to the above point, if a service user is harmed during an intervention, the same member of staff may again find themselves being investigated or disciplined for having harmed a service user by using force that was not, in the eyes of the employer, *'the minimum amount of force required'*.

If we are to be blunt, but also to the point, the promotion of *'minimum force'* normally derives from sources not competent in their understanding of the law in relation to the use of physical force. The dangerous dichotomy here is that the source is also likely to be the same one that will be responsible for the choice of the system of training used, choice of training provider, and any investigation and management in relation to the operational use of force within the organisation. This can (and has) led to staff being investigated and disciplinary action taken against them. Some have even been 'charged' with 'criminal offences' that they cannot be charged with. This can result in staff being wrongly accused, being inappropriately recommended for disciplinary action, or worse, wrongly referred to a 'list' as they are considered to pose a risk to children. In the latter case, work prospects can be affected, and ultimately someone is psychologically damaged and traumatised by the whole process that should never have occurred in the first place.

The fact that *'minimum force'* exists at all, and has gained such widespread acceptance simply boils down to what we refer to as *The King's new clothes syndrome.*

So where does the myth of minimum force have its origins?

To start with *'minimum force'* does not exist in statute or common law, and it is not mentioned in the Children Act 1989 either. However, in spite of this, the use of these words permeate numerous departmental policy and guidance in relation to the use of physical force, and many staff working in a diverse range of occupations are trained and instructed that they can only use *'minimum force'* when defending themselves or physically controlling a service user.

In short the wording *'minimum force'* appears to be a police invention. To further prove this point, the Metropolitan Police's Good Practice Guide to Officer Safety, produced by the Directorate of Public Affairs June 1995 states:

"No mention of minimum force is made in statute or common law; indeed this term appears to be a police invention."

In a paper published by the Criminal Law review in 1990 P.A.J. Waddington, Ph.D., Director of Criminal Justice Studies at the University of Reading, stated that *"the principle of 'minimum force' goes beyond, and is more restrictive than, what the law requires"*, which is that we all may use reasonable force in the defence of ourselves and/or others etc.

How does this sit with regard to the 'Welfare' or 'Paramount' Principle owed to the Child or other vulnerable person?

As you already know the 'Welfare', or 'Paramount' principle promotes the best interest of the child. For example, Section 1 (1)(a) of The Children Act 1989 states that: *"When the Court determines any question with respect to the upbringing of a child the child's welfare shall be the court's paramount consideration."*

In Article 3 (1) of the United Nations Convention on the Rights of the Child (Best Interests of the Child) states that: *"In all actions concerning children, whether undertaken by public or private social welfare institutions, courts of law, administrative authorities, or legislative bodies, the best interests of the child shall be a primary consideration."*

However, when considering these issues there is also the matter of competency to consider. For example, Article 3(3) of the United Nations Convention on the Rights of the Child (Best Interests of the Child) also states:

*"State parties shall ensure that the institutions, services and facilities responsible for the care or the protection of children shall conform with the standards established by **competent authorities**, particularly in the area of safety, health, in the number and suitability of their staff as well as **competent supervision**."*

Therefore, consistent with the *'Welfare'*, or *'Paramount'* principle, with regard to the best interests of the child, there could be circumstances when the application of a high degree of force may be necessary in order to minimise the overall likelihood of a greater harm occurring to a vulnerable person. This would be consistent with the concept of reasonable force.

However, if staff, who have responsibility for the welfare of vulnerable people, believe (or have been led to believe) that they are only allowed to *'apply the minimum amount of force'* then we could end up with situations whereby vulnerable children (and indeed vulnerable staff) are placed at unnecessary risk. This may be because the need to use force has not been minimised by the application of suitable and sufficient risk reduction and/or management controls, including adequate staffing levels.

As a result, when the need to use force arises, staff believing that they can only use *'minimum force'*, may resort to the use of ineffective physical techniques that fail to prevent harm by not effectively controlling a vulnerable person. As a result the margin for error increases and people are hurt.

If this occurs because of the misinterpretation and inference imposed on staff of what *'minimum force'* means, then the best interests of the vulnerable child become second to the best interests of staff, who are more concerned about not being disciplined by managers. These managers, in turn, may themselves have an incompetent understanding of what the law, specifically the law in relation to the use of physical force, and what it actually means. In short, in clear breach of Article 3(3) of the United Nations Convention on the Rights of the Child, the standards and supervision with regard to the best interest of the child are improperly understood and incorrectly implemented.

To conclude those persons responsible for the strategic and operational use of force within the organisation or department need to ensure that they not only appoint competent people, train staff to a competent standard, but also ensure that their policies and procedures are competently constructed by accurately reflecting what the law requires and provides.

Chapter 9
Acts v Omissions

In Chapter 4, we looked at the confusion that is created as to whether or not staff are allowed to stop a child leaving a care home, even if they believe that the child is likely to be placed at risk of harm. If you remember we mentioned that we regularly come across staff believing (or in some cases actually being told) that they are actually not allowed to stop the child from leaving and as such, expose the child to the risk of imminent or likely foreseeable harm.

In addition we know of some agencies who actively discourage staff from doing just that on the basis that they are not trained—thus preventing staff from taking some form of action. In addition other reasons then come into play, for example, fear of prosecution possibly being the most prominent—should staff attempt to do something and get it wrong. However, if this is the case, doesn't the very act of inactivity—*'not-acting'* or *'failing to act when one should*—create a liability in itself by allowing the harm to happen or continue?

To understand this, we need to understand the difference between acts and omissions in terms of how the law views them.

The difference between 'acts' and 'omissions'.

In the case of *Speck* (1977) a man was charged with committing an act of gross indecency with a child. The evidence was that an 8 year-old girl placed her hand on the man's trousers over his penis. The male adult allowed the hand to remain there for some minutes, causing him to have an erection. In this case, the Court of Appeal held that the adult's failure (omission) to remove the child's hand amounted to an invitation to the child to continue with the act. The Court held that the inactivity by the male adult in those circumstances amounted to an 'omission,' that by default, constituted an invitation to the child to commit an indecent act. It also recognised that failure of the adult to put an end to the child's touching was, in itself, an intentional act based on the intentional omission not to do what a responsible adult should have done in those circumstances.

In short, if we omit to intentionally act, to do what we know we ought to do, and that omission leads to a harm that could have been avoided—we run the risk of being held liable for the harm caused.

In the case of Costello v Chief Constable, a female police officer was attacked in a police cell by a young woman whom she had arrested for absconding from a care home. The male inspector accompanying the female officer did nothing to help her, and as a result, she was injured. The female officer successfully sued her employer (the Chief Constable of Police) for a breach of the duty of care owed to her, based on the fact that her male colleague acted negligently. This breached the duty of care owed to her by failing to come to her assistance, which, if he had have done, might have prevented or reduced the severity of the attack and the resultant harm she suffered.

In short the omission (the failure to assist) on behalf of her male colleague became an act of negligence for the organisation.

Let us look at another example a little closer to home. If we were to physically restrain someone, that would be an act. In short we have taken an action. We will have done something. However, if we did not restrain someone when we should have, for example, to prevent a vulnerable person harming themselves or others, and that failure to *'assist'* or *'go to their rescue'* led to an injury that might not have occurred had the act of restraint taken

133

place—then we have possibly 'omitted' to do something that we should have done. In short, we and/or the employer, may be cited for negligence.

What about the use of physical force?

Again many staff, and indeed many organisations and their management, believe that they just cannot use physical force. This is even promoted by some inspectors in their subjective (and possibly incorrect) interpretation of the various Standards and Acts. Yet this is in itself a potential omission.

With regard to how much force can be used in such circumstances, we need to look to the 'Proportionality' standard that makes up one of the aspects of reasonableness.

Although the standard of 'Proportionality' is not a precise standard it is best defined in the following terms taken from Professor Andrew Ashworth's[13] book, *Principles of Criminal Law*:

> *"The standard of Proportionality is best defined as what is reasonably proportionate to the amount of harm likely to be suffered by the defendant, or likely to result if the forcible intervention is not made".*

Again, if we notice the wording it states

> *"...the amount of harm likely to be suffered by the defendant or likely to result **if the forcible intervention is not made**".*

This seems to impose and infer that we have to consider the risk of not acting, or failing to respond, and the resultant harm that could result from such an omission, especially where

---

13 Andrew Ashworth is the Vinerian Professor of English Law at the University of Oxford and a Fellow of All Souls College. He is one of the UK's leading criminologists..

such a harm or injury might not have occurred by the pro-active application of force.

Therefore, any agency that is responsible for the welfare of others should realise that promotion of *'no-restraint polices,'* for example, is advertising the fact that they are promoting the right for their staff to omit to do what they are possibly expected, and maybe even employed to do. If so, such an omission could very possibly end up as an act of negligence, don't you think?

Would it not be simpler and easier if we just told staff exactly what they can do, what is expected of them, as opposed to supplying them with a multitude of subjective reasons and opinions as to what they cannot do—which by default, will have omitted to tell them what they can do—an omission in itself.

This raises another point, which is that those individuals who are responsible for the training, monitoring and supervision of others, and who may have responsibility for developing safe systems of work, safe working practices and departmental/ organisational policy, must have a competent understanding of the law in their professional field in addition to their academic, theoretical and experiential knowledge base. Otherwise their biased subjectivity could give rise to blinkered liability, which could lead to knowledge-based errors that may lead to corporate liability.

Furthermore, a failure to do something which results in the unnecessary death of another may become a breach of Article 2(1) of the Human Rights Act 1998, especially if that death was foreseeable and could have been prevented.

No Restraint Policies

Recently we were asked to provide a quote for an organisation with regard to the delivery of breakaway training. The company concerned worked with adults with learning disabilities, who presented challenging behaviour. This manifested itself in a risk of harm to self or others, or in serious damage to property that would pose a risk of harm to the service users.

Whilst undertaking a brief training needs analysis with them, it became evident from the types of incidents that were occurring, and from discussions with staff—that they had previously the need on many occasions to physically intervene with regard to the duty of care owed to the service user. When Mark raised this point of fact, he was informed by the management of the organisation that they had in place a *'no restraint policy'*. When Mark asked why, he was informed that they (the organisation) did not want to promote the use of physical restraint since it was not necessary.

Mark then asked the following question: *"If it is not necessary to restrain, and staff are not doing it—why have a no restraint policy?"*

If you think about it, if there is no need to restrain then you don't need a policy. So why have a policy in place to formalise a procedure for something that is not required or foreseeable? However, on the other hand, if the policy is in place to actively discourage the use of physical restraint because staff are doing it, then the question has to be asked—what is the real intention of the policy?

You see, if staff are using restraint then it can only be for a number of reasons. These might be:

1.   To protect service users from harming themselves or others, or seriously damaging property; or

2.   To intentionally harm service users, i.e. staff are using restraint as a punishment or to teach service users a lesson; or

136

3. Staff are having to use restraint as a control measure because of lack of suitable and sufficient, and possibly more appropriate and effective, alternative control measures being in place.

If staff are using restraint to protect service users from harming themselves or others, or from seriously damaging property, where this is necessary, and this is being actively discouraged, this could lead to a breach of the duty of care owed to a service user—if a service user were to become injured or killed as a result of staff not being allowed to intervene. There is also a moral issue here. Is it right in our society to enforce a policy whereby staff are expected to stand back and watch a service user get injured, or even worse, killed? This can lead to states of learned helplessness where staff will 'learn' that they are not expected to do things that any reasonable person would expect someone in their position to be doing. This in turn can lead to increased levels of distress for staff.

Additionally, Human Rights legislation, in particular Article 2, makes it a requirement that all public authorities have a positive obligation to promote and preserve the right to life. Therefore, if a no-restraint policy resulted in staff omitting to use force, and that omission lead to a death that could have been prevented by the use of force in that situation, then the organisation could be potentially prosecuted for a breach of Article 2. Furthermore, the new inclusion of the Corporate Manslaughter and Corporate Homicide Act 2007, states that an organisation will be guilty of an offence if the way in which its activities are managed or organised causes a person's death. This amounts to a gross breach of a relevant duty of care owed by the organisation to the deceased. (More on that in Chapter 11).

Events and Causal Factors Analysis

During the course of our consultancy work with various organisations we use ECFA (Events and Causal Factors Analysis) as an effective means of identifying where failings could, or have, occurred. Although ECFA models are normally used for collating data in accident investigations, we have used them effectively as a risk assessment analysis tool to foresee possible systematic or causal factors that could lead to a risk being realised.

As a result we have, on more than one occasion, specifically identified that a few well-meaning CSCI and HSE inspectors, as well as many managers responsible for implementing training can, and have been, a causal or systematic factor in increasing risk, and therefore the resultant harm to those whom they are mandated to protect. This is because some inspectors and managers are actually giving incompetent advice to agencies on what systems of intervention, or indeed even what specific techniques may and may not be used, when they are not competent to do so.

Therefore, we thought it would be worthwhile writing a few lines to explain more clearly what an ECFA is and also how it can be used in ascertaining systematic and causal factors associated with risk.

An ECFA [Events and Causal Factors Analysis] is a method of collecting data from accident and incident investigations which is normally viewed as a chart to illustrate the events and causal factors that would have been involved in an incident and how these interrelate.

A simple ECFA Chart[14] can be seen in the following example which involves a number of events and factors that have led up to a child being harmed.

Primary Events

In this example the **Primary Events** leading up the harm are as follows:

---

14 Reference: Health and safety: risk management – Dr. Tony Boyle – IOSH Publications

- Children continuously attempt to leave the home and abscond, placing themselves at risk of abuse and harm;

- Staff don't stop the child leaving;

- The child is harmed.

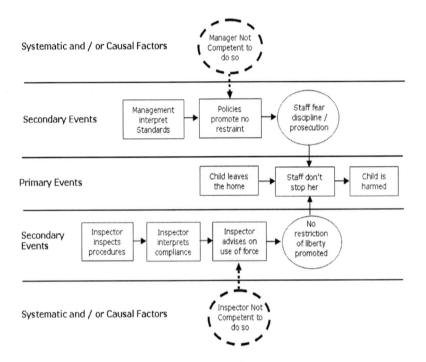

These are shown as a linear event in the row marked '**Primary Events**'.

Secondary Events

Other relevant events, known as '**Secondary Events**' are recorded above and below the row of 'Primary Events'. (They can be as many rows as possible but for this example only 2 rows have been shown to simplify the example.)

In the top row of '**Secondary Events**' we can see that:

- The management have interpreted the Care Home Standards to mean that they are not allowed to restrict a child's liberty should they attempt to abscond.

- As such they have produced 'no restraint' policies to ensure that staff do not stop children leaving the home, as this would constitute, based on their subjective interpretation, a breach of the Care Home Standards.

- This leads to staff fearing discipline or prosecution if they do attempt to stop a child leaving.

- As a result, children are not prevented from leaving the home, even if there is a risk of harm, as staff and management have the fear of discipline and prosecution at the forefront of their minds as opposed to the best interests of the child.

In the bottom row of '**Secondary Events**' we can see that:

- Inspectors assess the home to ensure compliance with the standards, as is part of their professional remit.

- The Inspector interprets the home's policies and procedures to ensure compliance with the Care Home Standards.

- Is satisfied that the 'no restraint policy' implemented by the home is consistent with the Care Home Standards (in fact the policy itself was implemented as a result of an inspector's advice and guidance on Standard compliance).

140

- Advises that staff should not use physical force to prevent a child leaving the home or even bolt a door temporarily as this would be an unlawful restriction of a child's liberty.

Systematic and Causal Factors

Systematic and Causal factors are referred to in ECFA as 'conditions' and are normally recorded above and below the relevant primary and secondary sequence of events. These are normally contained in 'oval shaped' boxes and connected by dotted lines/arrows.

It is normally usual to differentiate between 'systematic' and 'causal' contributory factors as follows.

Systematic Factors

Systematic is when the 'system' used is at fault resulting in reduced safety overall. For example, there is no formal safe system of working or safe working practices in place, risk assessments have not been undertaken for hazardous activities and staff are generally left to use their own 'common sense' to 'get on with it' as part of the job.

Causal Factors

A 'causal' factor is when failings take place due, in this case for example, to advice being given on the use of physical force by someone not competent in their knowledge base in that area. This can be due to systematic failings where people in certain 'positions' are expected to advise without proper competent guidance or training, or where the person has decided to act outside of the scope of their employed role by advising on issues that they are not competent in, but think that they know best.

In the above example, which is based on an actual incident investigation, where two care home staff were suspended for using force to prevent a child running into a busy road in an attempt to commit suicide, we found, by asking some very simple questions, that the managers and the inspectors competence in the specific area of physical force was subjective and not based on any competent understanding of the law, or indeed, the wider guidance available in their professional area of work.

We have simplified the process somewhat to give you hopefully a clearer understanding. There are also other H&S Models for investigation that we use, such as HSG65 and HSG48 for systematic and human factors which are worth knowing about.

A point of fact is that some individuals involved in the regulation and monitoring of children do not get training on the broader legal perspective, or the physiological and psychological aspects with regard to the use of physical force. As such, they need to be mindful that they may be giving polarised advice, based only on their interpretation of the Care Home Standards, which can lead to a liability for themselves and/or their departments.

Where the former would be regarded as a 'causal factor,' the latter would be a 'systematic failing' in terms of the inability to ensure that such individuals get competent training—not just training, but competent training.

Restraint attempted by a single individual

One question that arises in many conversations is whether a member of staff can restrain another individual on their own. For example, can a child care worker, working alone on a night shift, be legally allowed to physically intervene or interpose between two children fighting? Can a teacher on break duty physically interpose between two pupils fighting?

Sadly, these questions are normally driven by financial restrictions and departmental budgets, compounded by a lack of any approved code of practice or regulatory guidance.

The following therefore, is our professional view on the issue based on years of operational, training and coaching experience and a review of some the legislation and guidance on this issue.

Is it legal to restrain on my own?

It is not unlawful for any one individual to physically restrain another person on their own as no law prohibits it. However, as you already know, physical restraint is an activity that carries with it a degree of operational risk and, therefore, must be suitably and sufficiently assessed for risk. This is a requirement under various sections of the Health and Safety at Work etc Act 1974 and the supporting Management Regulations that we have already discussed.

This risk of any foreseeable injury (or even fatality) should be assessed and then eliminated or minimised by the provision of lawfully competent, appropriate and effective control measures, which may include training and seclusion (more on locking of doors later on). These control measures should be written down in formalised documentation to form the organisation's 'safe system of work'. Where physical restraint is a required control measure, it is important for the organisation to ensure that sufficient numbers of trained staff are available to undertake the activity.

Volume 4 of the Regulations accompanying the Children Act 1989 make this point clear. It states:

> "*Where children in homes have suffered particularly damaging experiences, and have difficultly developing the self-control or good personal relationships which diminish the need for physical restraint, it is important that sufficient, able staff are employed to ensure that the children are dealt with sensitively and with dignity.*"

Note the emphasis on *"sufficient, able staff are employed".* This requires that the employer has a duty to ensure to ensure that appropriate staffing levels are in place and that that staff are *"able"* (i.e., have the ability to do the skill to a competent level) so that if force has to be used on a child there are enough trained staff on duty to be able to handle the intervention competently, appropriately and effectively.

This is further emphasised by Sir Herbert Lamming's document: *'The Control of Children in the Public Care: Interpretation of the Children Act 1989 (S.S.I. 1997)'* where he states:

> *"Every effort should be made to secure the presence of other staff to ensure that any action taken is both safe and successful.*
>
> *It would be an error of judgement if a member of staff tried to restrain a young person without proper assistance and in so doing caused injury to himself or the young person because the intervention was handled ineptly."*

In addition, should an injury occur as a result of someone attempting physical restraint on their own, a court may look for compliance with any secondary legislation, safe working practices or guidance issued by other agencies and as to whether such guidance was sought and/or considered by the employer. Various guidance exists with regard to restraint and some examples are listed below:

Royal College of Nursing—Principles of Good Practice Requires:

> *"A policy relevant to the client group and setting which sets out when restraint, holding or containing may be necessary and how it may be done.*

Sufficient numbers of staff who are trained and confident in safe and appropriate techniques and in alternatives to restraint, holding and containment."

Health & Safety Executive Letter dated 12 May 2000.

Prior to training one NHS Trust's Security Team, Mark wrote to the Health and Safety Executive to gauge their perspective on the issue of control and restraint. In the final paragraph of the HSE reply they highlight the need for a suitable and sufficient risk assessment to be carried out and that adequate training is provided.

All of the guidance available suggests that it would be a serious error of judgement for any individual (or company) to suggest, or worse encourage, physical restraint to be attempted by a single person. Such advice would be contrary to any guidance issued by various 'responsible' authorities on the matter.

Therefore, to answer the initial question should employers rely on their employees common law rights in absence of any forthcoming training and guidance, we would say that they can, but they would be very naive to do so. In short, if the employee is expected to deal with issues that arise out of the nature of their employed role then the issue is whether or not the risk of such an encounter is foreseeable in the working environment and the employed role the member of staff finds themselves in. If the answer is yes; then the employer has an absolute duty to ensure that the risk is properly assessed and appropriate control measures implemented, including training.

Chapter 10
Positional Asphyxia

During the past decade and a half there has been increased awareness about dangers associated with particular forms of restraint. Deaths in police custody have, for example, led to positional asphyxia being far more widely acknowledged as a risk factor associated with physical restraint.

Definition of Positional Asphyxia

> *"Death which results from a body position that interferes with the ability to breathe. Positional asphyxia is a recognised cause of death."*

> *Police Complaints Authority -Policing Acute Behavioural Disturbance - Revised Edition, March 2002*

Positional asphyxia normally occurs when compression of the trunk limits chest movements preventing the diaphragm moving up and down between the chest and the abdomen, thereby impairing breathing. As Dr. Nat Carey, one of the UK's leading pathologists stated in a Police Complaints Seminar (now the IPCC) in May 2000

> *"If you put someone with a beer belly on their front you will squeeze their abdominal contents such that the diaphragm is relatively ineffective."*

The Legal Perspective

Under Section 3 of the Health and Safety at Work etc Act 1974 it states that:

"It shall be the duty of every employer to conduct his undertaking in such a way as to ensure so far as is reasonably practicable that persons not in his employment are not exposed to risks to their health and safety."

This is an absolute duty, so the employer must do whatever is reasonably practicable to eliminate or reduce such risks. Now, as many of you will know *"reasonably practicable"* equates to cost v risk. The higher the foreseeable risk the less cost becomes an argument. This has implications for issues such as adequate staffing levels and competent staff training where employers may argue that cost is an issue. However, if not providing adequate numbers of suitably trained staff leads to an injury or death that could have been prevented, the employer could arguably be prosecuted for a breach of Section 3.

With regards to the prevention of positional asphyxia, Part 1 of Article 2 of the Human Rights Act is particularly relevant. As you have already read, Part 1 of Article 2 is an 'Absolute Right'. What that means is that it cannot be derogated against (detracted from). This means that all public authorities, be they public or private companies undertaking a public function, such as transporting prisoners, managing private care homes, etc., must promote the positive obligation to preserve life where the risk to life is foreseeable. This particular Article has been described as one of the most fundamental provisions of the whole Act.

As a result issues that may arise in our Courts may include:

- Whether the planning surrounding the use of lethal force eradicates as far as possible the chances of loss of life;

- Whether the training of staff to recognise and deal with life-threatening situations is adequate;

- And whether training in safer ways of restraining violent individuals complies with the Convention standard.

What are the Risks?

Police Research Series: Paper 26—Deaths In Police Custody: Learning The Lessons (1998)

The Home Office Police research Group (PRG) was formed in 1992 to carry out and manage research in the social and management sciences relevant to the work of the police service. The group carried out a study of deaths in police custody drawing on official records from enquiries into 277 deaths, which occurred between January 1990 and December 1996. An extract of their findings associated to restraint are highlighted below.

Deaths that may have been associated with police restraint accounted for only 6 per cent of deaths and, in many of these cases, other potential causal factors also came into play such as the detainee's underlying physical and medical condition, as well as the circumstances of their arrest.

The report went on to comment that the presence of drugs may have played a part in some of the deaths with which police restraint may have been associated, primarily by increasing the person's readiness to resist arrest and/or reducing their susceptibility to pain.

In many of these cases, detainees were recorded as reacting violently to arrest. Such a reaction may place a detainee at greater risk whilst officers restrain them, and once they have been restrained. Furthermore, the combination of the way in which the detainee was held after arrest and other factors such as their size and medical condition, earlier physical exertion, or consumption of drugs or alcohol, featured in many of the deaths where restraint may have been a factor.

The second largest grouping of causal factors related to the detainee's medical conditions as recorded in the data studied by the group. Severe or chronic medical conditions apparently caused 81 deaths, or 29 per cent of the total. In many of these cases the detainee's condition was probably related to long-term, high risk behaviours, such as alcoholism.

Two conditions in particular were common:

1. Heart problems and

2   Head injuries.

Apart from four people who died as a result of epilepsy, the detainees dying from medical conditions were considerably older than in other cases. Importantly, however, in a few of these cases, the post mortem suggested that officers might have mistaken signs of illness for drunkenness. In total, 22 of the 27 people who died from a head injury were suspected of being drunk. Most of these people were later found to have consumed alcohol, but the records suggested that the head injury that actually caused their death was frequently missed.

The third main category of deaths focused on whether police restraint was a factor and concerned those deaths apparently associated with the actions of other individuals. This was the smallest category, representing only 22 (8 per cent) of the 275 deaths categorised by the study, and was broken down into the following sub-categories:

1. 16 cases where the death may have been associated with police actions (the main focus of this section)

2. 3 cases where the death may have been associated with doctors or medics actions; and;

3.   3 cases where the death may have been associated with the actions of other third parties.

For the purpose of this section we will look at the findings in the report that relate to the 16 cases (6 per cent of the 275 deaths categorised) that may have been associated with the actions of the police and, in particular, to the ways in which officers restrained the detainees at the time of their arrest and once they were in custody.

The study group uses the word "associated," rather than "caused." In some of these cases, it appears there may have been a degree of fault either on the part of the officers, or in terms of whether they had been given the right guidance. In other cases, the records suggested that the officers may have injured the deceased by *accident* (for instance, by falling on the detainee during a scuffle).

However, the report indicates that such deaths were rare— representing only 6 per cent of all the deaths investigated or approximately 1.4 deaths for every one million people arrested for notifiable offences over the seven-year period.

There were, however, some key features common to most cases:

- All but two of the detainees were recorded as having resisted arrest and "struggled" with the police, and in a majority of cases a "violent" struggle was described.

- All but one detainee was restrained with physical restraint and equipment combined.

- Where it was recorded, officers appeared to have reacted quickly and correctly when they realised the condition of the detainee, by attempting resuscitation and calling for an ambulance. In three cases, however the deceased was taken to the police station and "carried" into the custody suite.

In some cases, it was apparent from the records and Coroner's inquests that the police actions were either accidental or unavoidable.

In nine cases it appeared that the police applied restraint in a way that may have contributed to the detainee's deaths. In all these cases, however, some other factor was also present. It is conceivable that these other factors meant that, in some cases, the detainees were more vulnerable in the face of restraint. For example:

- In one case, the pathologist suggested that the drug taken would have increased the need for oxygen, magnifying the effects of any restriction of the windpipe. The records reported the comments as follows: *"Cocaine is a very powerful local anaesthetic which reduces sensations of pain and the anaesthetic weakens the heartbeat"*. In normal use, people can hallucinate, become agitated, and if one tries to restrain them, they may become quite violent. Because of the anaesthetic effect of cocaine, the forceful actions of the user are not limited by pain, thus enabling the user to act more violently. Cocaine puts the heart under stress and increases the need for oxygen. In the case of a person who is under the influence of cocaine and who is struggling violently, the demand for oxygen is increased enormously, so mildly or incompletely pressing on the windpipe could be enough in those circumstances to be fatal.

- In another case, obesity was noted as increasing the deceased's vulnerability to restraint.

- In another case, the pathologist recorded that the detainee suffered acute exhaustive mania. This condition, also known as excited delirium, can be caused by drugs, alcohol, a psychiatric illness or some combination of these. Someone suffering from it may ignore pain and continue to struggle beyond exhaustion—placing themselves at considerable risk if restrained by officers.

For some detainees therefore, restraint, coupled with the vulnerability of the detainee, contributed to their death.

However there were three other cases which caused greatest concern to the study group. In these, restraint failure (ineffective restraint) appears to have been a key cause of death.

In total, thirteen cases appeared to involve the failure of police restraint. These thirteen cases were split almost evenly between six cases where the restraint failure occurred during a struggle, and seven cases where it occurred because of the way in which the detained was restrained after arrest.

The six cases where detainees were apparently injured during struggle, is broken as follows:

- In three cases police restraint was apparently related to the asphyxia from which the detainee died. In the first two of these, an officer had applied a neck-hold, whilst in the third it was not clear what exactly had caused the asphyxiation.

- In two cases officers may have applied force, with a baton, in a way that apparently resulted in serious injuries to the detainee.

- In one other case, the detainee died after a "violent struggle". This person apparently suffered acute exhaustive mania, which may have meant that they continued to struggle despite the increasing use of restraint by officers (including the use of CS-spray).

These cases highlighted the importance of restraint training for officers in the use of equipment and its combination with physical restraint. In particular, they demonstrated the dangers if officers applied too much pressure to a detainee's neck whilst trying to hold them. One case highlighted the need for officers to be aware of the potential for detainees' medical or psychological conditions to place them at greater risk if restrained. Officers may find they have to "back off" from restraining a detainee if it becomes apparent that they have such a condition.

The seven cases where restraint after arrest appeared to have been mishandled included:

- One case in which police officers were assisting immigration officials, where the detainee apparently suffocated after tape was placed around their head.

- Six cases where the restraint may have led to a condition termed postural or positional asphyxia. Past research, particularly in the US, had suggested that such deaths could occur where an individual was held down or placed in a prone position and restricted in their movement—either because their hands were handcuffed behind them or because someone was on top of them, holding them down.

Referring to postural asphyxia, one pathologist noted it is a particular danger where the individual being restrained is "obese".

The recommendations made by the report stated that officers should avoid placing detainees in a neck-hold, or holding them face down for a long period, or applying any weight on their back. They should also avoid leaving them unattended in any position that might restrict their breathing. Even if the position itself does not present a danger, the detainee may be suffering from a medical condition or the effects of substance abuse and these, combined with the restraint, could place their life in danger.

One other lesson learned was the need for close supervision of detainees once they are restrained:

- In two cases, the detainee was placed "flat out' or "face down" in the back of the police van and was not, apparently, accompanied when in transit.

- In another case a detainee, having been placed "face down" in the police van, was not accompanied by the doctor who had sedated the person.

These examples highlighted the need for officers always to pay careful attention to the physical condition of people they have restrained – particularly where they have resisted restraint and have been held in a way that might have restricted their breathing pattern. In addition, they illustrate the dangers of conveying such restrained detainees unsupervised.

The study also provided some evidence that:

- The detainees who died and who had taken drugs were more likely to have been restrained on arrest;

- In many of the cases where the detainee's death may have been associated with the actions of the police, the detainee was recorded as reacting violently to arrest; and

- The presence of drugs, or a violent reaction to arrest may have made the detainees more vulnerable to the impact of restraint when being arrested—increasing their chances of injury or death.

Officers should, therefore, take particular care when restraining anyone they suspect of having taken drugs, or who reacts violently to arrest.

In summary, therefore, the following risk factors should be understood:

- In some cases death follows a violent struggle in which officers claim to fear for their own safety;

- There is a particular danger if the restrained person is obese;

- Is placed in a prone position;

- Has their hands immobilised behind their backs; and/or

- Pressure or weight is applied on their backs.

Other Risk Factors that can cause death:

- Use of Neck-holds.

- Especially on the Carotid sinus or vagus nerve.

- Any technique that restricts breathing, diaphragmatic and lung function.

- Lack of supervision post restraint.

Neck Holds should not be used because they:

- Elevate blood pressure;

- Stimulate the sympathetic nervous system;

- Cause sudden drop in blood pressure; and

- May result in death.

Actions required to reduce the risk of death:

- Restrict the use of prone restraint unless absolutely necessary for control—*"The prone position should be avoided if at all possible and the period that someone is restrained in the prone position needs to be minimised."* —*Nat Cary, PCA Seminar, May 2000*

- If possible, contain rather than restrain.

- Once controlled, move subject onto their side, or into a seated position as soon as possible.

- Monitor breathing and pulse rates and seek medical examination immediately—especially if the subject should become very passive or calm.

- If possible, avoid the situations in which prolonged restraint and prolonged struggling become necessary.

- If the person has to be restrained avoid pressing down on the trunk.

"The amount of time that restraint is applied is as important as the form of restraint and the position of the detainee. Prolonged restraint

and prolonged struggling will result in exhaustion, possibly without subjective awareness of this, which can result in sudden death."

—Nat Cary, PCA Seminar, May 2000

Hartford Courant Database

The Hartford Courant database was collated by investigative reporters concerned at the increasing, yet invisible, number of restraint related fatalities in the USA. This lists a total of 142 deaths from 1988 to 1998. The ages of the deceased range from 6 to 84. Although the published data lacks detail, and codification presents problems, it is possible to identify certain trends. Around 54 per cent of the cases cited contain no information on the method/type or position of restraint. Of the remainder, 50 per cent were associated with a wide variety of factors in which the mechanical restraint of elderly people featured prominently. However:

- 31 per cent involved restraint in a prone position;

- A further 7 per cent involved some kind of floor restraint;

- 11 per cent involved " take downs " to the floor; and

- 3 per cent involved basket holds.

In all, taking the restrained person to the floor was implicated in around 49 per cent of cases where the method of restraint was specified.

NAMI (the National Alliance for the Mentally Ill)

A subsequent summary of reports, collated by the National Alliance for the Mentally Ill (NAMI, 2000), reported 58 recorded incidents from October 1998. 13 clearly involve fatalities.

- Of these 31 per cent involved prone restraint;

- 5 per cent taking to the floor;

- 15 per cent basket holds; and

- The methods used were unknown in 39 per cent of cases.

There has also been greater emphasis placed upon avoiding any techniques that may impair breathing, diaphragmatic movement and lung function. In March 2000, for example, the Department of Health issued draft guidance on the use of physical interventions for staff working with children and adults with learning difficulties and/or autism. The document says that agency policies should clearly describe unacceptable practices including avoiding methods of intervention which restrict breathing, or impact upon the person's airways, an example given is:

> 10.4 *"...using "basket holds" where the person's arms are drawn tight across their chest by a person standing behind them."*

In spite of this, the technique described above continues to be taught as a primary method of intervention on several training programmes relating to physical intervention with children. Given the high percentage of children and young people who suffer from asthma and other breathing related disorders, this is particularly worrying.

Whilst specific research into dangers associated with the physical restraint of children and young people is limited, the Scottish Office produced the "Children's Safeguard Review" in 1997, which addressed some of these issues. Common sources of injuries were said to include:

- Excessive staff numbers;

- Failure to co-ordinate the intervention of staff;

- Failure to give explicit protection to the head of the person being restrained;

- The application of weight or pressure to the back or abdomen;

- Failure to control descents; and

- Wrist injury.

Furthermore, the report states that some techniques may also be more likely to compromise the dignity of the young people and careful consideration needs to be given to the use of certain techniques including:

- All techniques which involve "flooring"

- Techniques which involve holding the trunk such as bear hugs

- Techniques which involve straddling a young person on the ground

- Techniques which involve pain compliance such as wrist locks

- Techniques which push a young person's face into the floor.

The case of Zoe Fairley highlights these issues and the following is an extract of the article that was published in the Daily Mail newspaper on Wednesday 24th August 1997. Although not a child, her death highlights some of the hazards and risks that we should all be aware of when restraining anyone.

'Handicapped girl died 'as care
workers pinned her to the floor'

"A woman was crushed to death as four care workers held her face down on the floor, an inquest heard yesterday. Zoe Fairley, 21, who was mentally handicapped, had been restrained for 30 minutes when she suddenly became weak and stopped breathing. She had flown into a tantrum after arriving at the Social Services hostel where she sometimes stayed.

The emergency services were called but attempts to revive her failed, She died from suffocation, her injuries similar to those of the Hillsborough disaster and mining accidents, the hearing at York was told.

Coroner Donald Coverdale said that although no one was on trial at the inquest, the jury had to 'determine whether there is evidence of foul play or abuse'.

Miss Fairley had been born with a congenital defect and had suffered from behavioural and learning difficulties all her life. She lived with her parents Brian and Kathleen but had become increasingly difficult to look after. To give them a break she started staying overnight at the Howe Hill respite care unit in York.

On September 13, 1995, the day of her death, she became wheezy after walking the short distance to Howe hill and sat down. Then the tantrum started. Rachel Snowball, group leader at Howe hill, said Miss Fairley kicked over a coffee table and ran at her, her hands punching the air. Miss Snowball and another carer Malcolm Brooks forced her to the ground. Miss Snowball said: 'We had to call for more help because we were losing control. Zoe was incredibly strong.'

Miss Fairley was restrained by two of the workers putting pressure on each shoulder, one putting pressure on her legs and the other pressing down on her buttocks, said Miss Snowball. 'After some time Zoe seemed to have calmed down so we gradually got off her one by one,' she added. 'She did not move—which was not uncommon —but we soon realised something was wrong when her left hand looked blue and her arm was limp.'

Kathleen Fairley wept as she told the inquest that her daughter, despite her handicap, was 'very loving'. But she had become increasingly violent. 'Zoe was like a little girl in an adult body,' said Mrs Fairley.

When her daughter began attending Howe Hill, she signed a form agreeing to the regime of control there. The four-step procedure began with 'ignoring' bad behaviour, then moved on to 'redirecting her attention elsewhere', then 'shepherding' her away and finally restraining her on the ground.

She added: 'If we had known four people would hold her down, we probably wouldn't have gone through with it.' Miss Fairley was described as powerful and muscular despite being just 4ft 10in. She weighed just under 14 stone. Home Office pathologist Professor Michael Greensaid the cause of death was asphyxia due to compression of the trunk.

Restraint-related deaths in this country were 'very rare indeed' he added, and it was only in the last 12 months that the dangers of the 'prone' position had been appreciated by experts."

The above case highlights a number of hazards associated with the activity of physical restraint, namely: excessive staff numbers, failure to co-ordinate the activity, restraint being allowed to go on for extended periods of time (restraint failure), the use of the 'prone' position, the absolute reliance on non-harmful methods of control and the absolute exclusion of more restrictive locks and pain-compliance techniques. It is a perverse state of affairs when a restraint involving 'non-harmful methods of control' ends up harming someone to the extent that they die.

It would be very sad if more restrictive, and possibly even pain-compliance, techniques were deliberately avoided in this instance out of a basic desire not to intentionally cause harm. The use of such a technique may have been effective in gaining control of the situation more quickly, and although it would have caused some pain in the short-term, it may have prevented a greater harm from occurring, by saving the young woman's life.

It concerns us that there are now a number of associations who advocate absolutely that pain-compliance techniques are not to be used and these seem to be supported by certain 'Standards Inspectors' acting as enforcement officers. Our main concern here is that although their focus appears to be primarily the welfare of the service user, their competence in making such omissions needs to be challenged as they may, in certain cases, be placing the service user and member of staff at risk of greater harm, and it will certainly lead to increasing claims against the organisation for injury due to negligence. From a legal perspective, they may also fall foul of the law by failing to preserve the positive obligation to preserve life.

Gareth Myatt: Death due to Restraint

More recently the death in custody of 15 year-old Gareth Myatt has again brought the issue of restraint into the spotlight.

Gareth was a 15 year old child from Stoke on Trent. He was small for his age, being only 4 foot 10 inches tall and weighing 6 1/2 stone. Gareth died after being restrained by three adult officers at the privately run Rainsbrook Secure Training Centre on 19 April 2004. During the restraint Gareth lost consciousness and is said to have died from "positional asphyxia" after choking on his own vomit.

What is unique about Gareth Myatt's death is the fact that he was the first child ever to die in a privately run Secure Training Centre (STC) and is the only child to have died following restraint here in the UK. In the US, however, children have been dying at an alarming rate for years

Gareth was restrained under a Home Office and YJB (Youth Justice Board) approved restraint technique known as the 'seated double embrace'. This type of restraint was part of a series of techniques approved by Home Office ministers as part of the Physical Control in Care (PCC) system of restraint. On police advice, the 'seated double embrace' technique was withdrawn from use following his death and as yet has not been reinstated.

Although the jury in the inquest returned a verdict of accidental death, due to *"insufficient evidence"*, it made sweeping criticisms about the conduct of the Youth Justice Board, saying it had failed to adequately assess the safety of the restraint used on Gareth.

Amongst other factors, the inquest into Gareth's death scrutinised:

1. How such a method of restraint was given ministerial and/or governmental approval for use, (a point all managers of public and private agencies commissioning training should now seriously begin to bear in mind!);

2. The monitoring, auditing and reviewing of the system of restraint used, (PCC) and if potential risks were identified;

3. How staff were chosen to be trained in the system
    of restraint (staff ability and competence).

Following the verdict, Gareth's mother, Pam Wilton, said: "What I have heard has deeply upset, angered and shocked me. I loved Gareth so much and my life will never be the same. When he went to Rainsbrook I expected him to get the help he needed. At the end of all of this he is still dead and no-one has been held accountable."

Deborah Coles, co-director of campaign group Inquest, which has backed Gareth's case, called the verdict a "shameful indictment" of the Youth Justice Board's failure to protect children in custody. She said: "The jury accept that these failures directly caused Gareth's death. His death was entirely preventable and was a disaster waiting to happen.

Chapter II
The Corporate Manslaughter
&
Corporate Homicide Act 2007

The Corporate Manslaughter and Corporate Homicide Act became part of UK Law on 26 July 2007. Under the new legislation an organisation will be guilty of an offence if the way in which its activities are managed or organised causes a person's death, and amounts to a gross breach of a relevant duty of care owed by the organisation to the deceased.

In short, companies and organisations can be prosecuted where there has been a gross failing, throughout the organisation, in the management of health and safety that has resulted in fatal consequences

Implications regarding the use for physical force by employed staff.

What is interesting is that the new Act also includes an amendment to include deaths in custody, and this is particularly well-timed if we consider the recent cases of Gareth Myatt and Adam Rickwood. This amendment will allow organisations to be prosecuted where death results from the use of physical restraint, particularly where companies and organisations have failed to manage the risks associated with the activity such as ensuring that the training is carried out in such a way as to minimise the risk to loss of life—already a requirement also under Article 2(1) of the Human Rights Act 1998.

Under the new Act, an organisation is guilty of the offence of corporate manslaughter, if the way in which any of the organisation's activities are managed by the senior managers, is a substantial element in the breach that:

a) Causes a person's death; and

b) Amounts to a gross breach of a relevant duty of care owed by the organisation to the deceased.

The interpretation of "employee"

Under the new Act the interpretation of *"employee"* means:

"an individual who works under a contract of employment or apprenticeship (whether express or implied and, if express, whether oral or in writing),"....

This means that the term *"employee"* includes all staff, full-time, part-time, casual and/or voluntary. Therefore, if *"employees"* were expected to use physical force, either by a formal condition of contract, or where, even in the absence of a formal condition of contract the inference was *"implied"*, the company or organisation will be responsible for any resultant death, particularly where a death results from a failure in the way in which the staff or the operational use of force is managed, i.e., by inadequate staffing levels, lack of training, or worse, provision of incompetent training that fails to manage the risk posed (i.e., training that does not work in it's operational context).

The new Act seems to draw together various elements of Human Rights and Health and Safety at Work legislation, acting as a means of prosecution should death occur which could have been prevented by having in place a suitable and sufficient risk management strategy aimed at promoting the right to life, especially where a risk to life is known to exist.

The recent deaths of Gareth Myatt and Adam Rickwood have highlighted the risks associated with the use of force with vulnerable individuals. However, these are not isolated cases and it is worth noting that since 1990, twenty-nine children have died from restraint in custody in England and Wales.

Therefore, as a direct result of this new legislation senior management of companies and organisations will need to review their use of force procedures and systems of intervention (defence) and breakaway (self-defence) to ensure they do not fall foul of the new offences created by the Act, now that it is in force. In addition senior management should not just 'buy-in' training, even if it is being marketed as 'approved' or 'accredited' training by a particular agency, but use due diligence to find out whether the training actually complies with what the law requires. If not, senior management responsible for the commissioning of training may find themselves defending a charge of Corporate Manslaughter in England, Wales and Northern Ireland and Corporate Homicide in Scotland.

> *"There are huge numbers of managers out there who understand all too well the risks that their staff take to make the system work. And as long as the system is working and no one is seriously injured, they will turn a blind eye to the irregular, and in some cases, dangerous and illegal practices that are being used. Yet, should someone be seriously injured, or even die, then questions will be raised by the very people who know all too well what is happening and why. For what purpose? To cover their backs—and in some cases this means that their backs are covered at the expense of the very staff who make an unworkable system work."*

> *[Extracted from 'Managing the Monkey—How to Defuse the Conflicts That Can Lead to Violence in the Workplace by Mark Dawes—November 1999].*

After almost 10 years of debate, and 7 years from the publication of the book *Managing the Monkey,* the Government finally implemented the Corporate Manslaughter and Corporate Homicide Act on the 26th July this year.

This means that Courts will now be able to find an organisation guilty of the new offence if someone has been killed as a result of the gross failure of its senior managers who have failed to ensure safe working practices for their employees.

This is referred to as a *"management failure"*—an approach that focuses on the arrangements and practices for carrying out the organisation's work, rather than any immediate negligent act by an employee (or potentially someone else) causing death.

As we have seen already an organisation will be guilty of the offence of corporate manslaughter if the way in which any of the organisation's activities are managed or organised by the senior managers:

a)   causes a person's death; and

b)   amounts to a gross breach of a relevant duty of care owed by the   organisation to the deceased.

Gross Breach

A gross breach is a breach of a duty of care by an organisation that falls far below what can reasonably be expected of the organisation in the circumstances.

To decide whether a 'gross breach' has taken place, the jury must consider whether the evidence shows that the organisation failed to comply with any relevant health and safety legislation or guidance. In addition, there are a number of other factors which the jury will also have to consider, such as whether or not senior managers sought to cause the organisation to profit from its failure, i.e., that they deliberately cut corners to reduce costs or boost profits.

Possible future implications

These new proposals have wide ranging implications and should be a wake up call for all members of senior management whose staff (employed or contracted) take risks on behalf of their company or who are exposed to the risk of violence as part of their employed role.

This includes all staff, where the inference is that they may have to use physical force, but are not given suitable and sufficient training which results in the death of the person being restrained. Furthermore, should a death occur due to a restraint being undertaken with inadequate staff numbers, the company or organisation may be open to charges of corporate manslaughter.

Companies found guilty of corporate manslaughter will face an unlimited fine, and the new Act also gives the courts power to impose a remedial order—which can already be imposed for health and safety offences—requiring the company to address the cause of the fatality.

The Gareth Myatt Inquest

In light of the Inquest into Gareth Myatt's death and the points debated with regard to The Corporate Manslaughter and Corporate Homicide Act 2007 in the House of Lords, all managers and directors of public and private agencies responsible for the custody and care of children in our society need to be mindful of the fact that:

1. All commissioning agencies need to apply their own due diligence when considering training providers and not primarily base their assumption that the training provider is competent on them having been 'Accredited' or 'Approved' by a particular agency.

2. Any training should be formally assessed for risk by a competent individual in order to minimise the risk of injury and loss of life so far as is reasonably practicable in line with Health and Safety legislation.

3. All training must comply with the Convention standard promoted by the Human Rights Act 1998 in promoting the positive obligation to preserve life and that positive steps have been taken to do so.

4. Staff expected to use physical restraint must be physically capable of doing the skills, and have the ability to apply the skills taught in realistic operational situations to a competent standard. This means that training providers need to have some formal criteria for assessing staff, and for making recommendations to managers of commissioning agencies with regard to those staff who cannot do the skill to the required competent standard, and not just 'pass' someone who has simply attended and completed the training.

5. Suitable and sufficient monitoring and supervision of staff must be undertaken by competent management. This would require a member of that management undertaking the same training as their staff so that they have first hand experience of the skill they are expected to oversee.

On 6th June 2000 Anthony Scrivener QC was the keynote speaker at the Annual Symonds Safety Lecture at the Institution of Civil Engineers. The lecture was entitled, 'Corporate and Personal Manslaughter: Where the Offence is—Let the Great Axe Fall.' His talk began with the following opening statement which sums up the situation beautifully:

> *"Although in this short address I will refer to the Government's new proposals for corporate manslaughter I would wish to drive home a clear message to all of those involved in the management of companies.*
>
> *Even without these reforms there is an unstoppable movement towards using the full force of the criminal law against companies and executives forming the management of companies where death or injury is caused by serious negligence.*
>
> *They are out to get you and that is the clear message you should take back with you from this meeting to your boardroom.*
>
> *If you ignore the trend then you do so at you peril."*
>
> *—Anthony Scrivener QC, Tuesday, 6th June 2000*

Endnote

We sincerely hope that you have enjoyed this book. It is intended to complement, *Understanding Reasonable Force*, written by Mark Dawes, published in 2006 and which is available on our web site at: www.nfps.info or also on Amazon.

At the start of this book we stated that the use of force with children and young people is an emotive subject, fraught with controversy and at times, built on myth and misinterpretation. If we have managed to clear some of these issues up for you the only thing that remains now is for you to do something with the additional knowledge that you have possibly gained.

The Janus Principle

Janus was a Roman God who had two faces, one at the front and one at the back so he could see both ways. He was the God of doors and gates and Janus' temple in Rome had two doors, one at the west end and one at the east end of the building. The concept was that as the day began and the day ended the sun would shine through Janus' temple. In the middle of the temple was a big statue of Janus with both faces of the statue facing each door.

The message that Janus carried was that those who fail to remember their history will often repeat it, and that is to say that we all learn by our past efforts. However, what Janus is also saying is that if we fail to learn from the lessons of the past we will continue to make the same mistakes in the future. However, one of the most important messages that we believe Janus was giving was that we should always face our future with new optimism, but not forget our past.

As adults we can become set in our ways. Our habits and our routines become part of our everyday occurrence and we tend to live to the limitations of our familiarity. Sometimes we settle for being less than what we can be, at the expense of our potential, because of the fear of losing what we have gained. But is that because we have choice or because we have no choice? Are our limitations primarily because of what we could lose or what we could gain?

This reminded me of the now famous words attributed to Nelson Mandella that were written by Marianne Williamson which states:

"Our deepest fear is not that we are inadequate. Our deepest fear is that we are powerful beyond measure. It is our light, not our darkness, that most frightens us. We ask ourselves, who am I to be brilliant, successful, talented and fabulous? Actually, who are you NOT to be? You are a child of God. Your playing small doesn't serve the world. There's nothing enlightened about shrinking so that other people won't feel insecure around you. We were born to make manifest the glory that is within us. It's not just in some of us; it's in EVERYONE! And as we let our own light shine, we unconsciously give other people permission to do the same. As we are liberated from our own fear, our presence automatically liberates others!"

All of us are better than we allow ourselves to be. Some of us spend so much time looking back that we fail to look positively to the future.

Some of you who have read this book will find reasons not to change. Some of you will find reasons to change. Your decision, either way, will be based on what you have experienced in the past combined with what you think you will expect from the future. Where the past outweighs the future you will not change. Where your future outweighs the past you will move forward. Either way your decision will define the direction of your future, and possibly also, the future of others in your care.

The Roman God Janus looks both ways and one of the messages taught is that it is good to remember our past so that we don't continually make the same mistakes in our future. But like Janus we need to be looking at and into a future that is as compelling as a sunset that offers us the dawn of a new day, with all of the new opportunities and hopes that each new day brings. Otherwise we simply look forward to living in the past!

We hope, therefore, that the facts and information contained in this book has in some way helped you sort out fact from fiction from a more wholesome, practical and functional perspective.

Here's to your future.

All the very best.

Mark Dawes and Deborah Jones.